A Child of the Fifties

The Autobiography: 1944-59

by

Terence Cant
(James Warden)

Grosvenor House
Publishing Limited

All rights reserved
Copyright © James Warden, 2018

The right of James Warden to be identified as the author of this
work has been asserted in accordance with Section 78
of the Copyright, Designs and Patents Act 1988

The book cover picture is copyright to James Warden

This book is published by
Grosvenor House Publishing Ltd
Link House
140 The Broadway, Tolworth, Surrey, KT6 7HT.
www.grosvenorhousepublishing.co.uk

This book is sold subject to the conditions that it shall not, by way of
trade or otherwise, be lent, resold, hired out or otherwise circulated
without the author's or publisher's prior consent in any form of binding or
cover other than that in which it is published and
without a similar condition including this condition being imposed
on the subsequent purchaser.

A CIP record for this book
is available from the British Library

ISBN 978-1-78623-181-9

Other Writing by James Warden

<u>Stories of Our Time</u>
Three Women of a Certain Age (2010)
The Age of Wisdom (2015)
Swinging in the Sixties (2016)

<u>Tales of Mystery and Imagination</u>
The Vampire's Homecoming (2011)
The First Rendlesham Incident (2017)

<u>Stories for Children</u>
The Great Gobbler and his Home Baking Factory at the North Pole (2010)
The One-eyed Dwarf (2012)

<u>Biography</u>
The Boy in the Photograph: Bill Pieri's autobiography (2014)

<u>Plays</u>
As I Walked Out One Midsummer Morning (2009)
(Adapted with the permission of Laurie Lee's estate)
Letters from a Boy in the Trenches (2015)

To my sister, Linda,
with whom I shared a childhood,

and my parents,
Walter Ernest Cant and Edna Florence Warden,
without whom nothing would have been possible.

Contents

	List of Photographs	ix
	Author's Note and Acknowledgements	xiii
1.	First Years	1
2.	The House in Turin Street	8
3.	Mother and Father	23
4.	The Wardens of Bath Street	45
5.	The Daveys of Westerfield	60
6.	School	82
7.	Playing Out and Pastimes	108
8.	Neighbours and the Neighbourhood	126
9.	Saturday Morning Pictures and Going Up Town	141
10.	Festivities and Holidays	156
11.	Moving Out	172

List of Photographs

Chapter 1
1. On the beach at Kilcreggan with Dad, 1947
2. On the beach at Kilcreggan with Mum, 1947
3. Outside the Nissen huts with Keith Nutter on our tricycles, 1947

Chapter 2
4. In the backyard at Turin Street, circa 1949
5. Linda's christening. From the left, Grandad and Nana Bathstreet, Grandad and Nana Westerfield, Dad, Beattie Barber, 1951

Chapter 3
6. Mum and Dad with Aunty Betty and her brother, Curly, who was Dad's best man, pre 1939
7. Studio photograph, circa 1945

Chapter 4
8. Nana and Grandad Bathstreet with Lorna, Edna, Irene, Fred and Eric
9. Nana and Grandad Bathstreet on a stroll along the Ipswich docks, 1935
10. Nana and Grandad Bathstreet

Chapter 5
11. Grandad and Nana Westerfield
12. Nana Westerfield with her father, 'Gaga' Frost, and Beattie Barber's sister-in-law, Lily, and Barry, outside Grandad's shed where he taught me to pluck pheasants

Chapter 6
13. Class photograph, Luther Road Junior School. I am second from left on the back row, John Hunt is sixth and Robert Harrison far right; Jacqueline Kitchen is in front of me and Janet Ostler stands to her left; Janet Squire is seated on the third row, far right; Micky Warren and Roland Collins are sitting cross-legged to the right of the board, 1955
14. My first *Rupert Annual*, 1948

Chapter 7
15. The *Rupert Annual* that contained the stories *Rupert, the Witch and Tabitha* and *Rupert in Trouble Again*, 1950

Chapter 8
16. As a Sea Scout, photographed in our backyard at Turin Street, 1956

Chapter 9
17. One of the serials that seized our imaginations at Saturday morning pictures, 1952
18. The first book I bought for myself, 1957

Chapter 10
19. Lorna, Edna, and Fred's families with Nana and Grandad Bathstreet on Felixstowe beach
20. On the beach at Dovercourt, 1949
21. Our caravan holiday at Kessingland, circa 1958
22. School photograph, Coronation Year, 1953
23. With Father Christmas, probably in Footman's Department Store, c 1949
24. With Linda on a visit to our godparents in Westcliffe

Chapter 11
25. In the garden of our new bungalow at Gleneagles Drive, 1958

26. Inspired by the Sherlock Holmes stories, I bought this book in 1957
27. Inspired by the Sherlock Holmes stories, I bought this book in 1958
28. On a field study trip from the Ipswich Civic College 1962

Author's Note and Acknowledgements

It was while writing my seventh novel, *The First Rendlesham Incident*, that I hit upon the idea of attempting an account of my childhood. Working with Bill Pieri on his autobiography may well have suggested the idea but it was researching the science fiction story, set in the summer of 1955, which gave it impetus.

Two books had been central to this research – *A 1950s Childhood: From Tin Baths to Bread and Dripping* by Paul Feeney and *Jam Tomorrow: Memories of Life in Postwar Britain* by Tom Quinn. To both these books I owe the jogging of my own memories. They, obviously, offer a more comprehensive approach than my own story and are well worth reading.

Once I started writing, the memories came thick and fast: one simply gave rise to another and the problem was one of selection rather than recall. I wanted to keep the book crisp and true. The writing took me back to the family, friends and places I had known, and it was this sense of place and person that took me forward. I have used family photographs, documents and personal accounts to provide an appreciation of time and occasion.

At different points in the narrative, I have reflected upon my childhood. The memories are recorded in plain type and the reflections in *italics*.

I have used the real names of the people I knew except when I might have caused embarrassment: in these cases I have used a pseudonym, and indicated as such.

I would like to thank my sister, Lindy Edwards, for reading the original manuscript and suggesting any memories we shared that I might have forgotten.

Chapter One
First Years

I am standing at the bottom of a roadside bank: it is steep. One of my legs is stretched along the slope, the other placed on the road and bearing my weight. I am helping another boy to reach the top of the bank, supporting him with my right hand. It is a hot day and the bank is dusty; the other boy slips. The heat in the air invades my nose. We are wearing close-fitting shorts and half-sleeved shirts. I have a clear memory of a seriousness of purpose. He has a mop of thick, black, curly hair. He has almost scaled the slope; his hand is clutching grass, and there is simply that final pull to the top.

I am three years old and standing on a bench. Someone is holding me and the sea wind is blowing through my hair. I am aware that we are on a boat because I can feel the distinctive movement and see the water. I can also smell the salt. Ahead is an open stretch of water and on the far shore some buildings. Is there spray on my face?

The top half of a stable door is open. From the hallway, I am watching the blue sky beyond. A giant bee flies in, blown by the summer wind. I watch it with innocent curiosity and I am stung. A bluebag is applied to the injury.

Standing outside the same door one day, I see a car approaching at speed. The dust from the road blows about the vehicle. As I watch, the car swings towards me and I leap clear, losing my plimsoll, which the car crushes. The car brakes to a sharp halt just in front of our door. I am laughing with my mother who rushes out to hold me. She is wearing a short-sleeved summer dress.

These are real memories, as distinct from ones handed down by parents and relations during family gatherings. They are recalled with the vividness of a child's early perceptions: I can smell and feel as well as see them. I have always loved boats and stable doors, and believe that affection stems from this time. Was this also the beginning of my love of women in summer dresses? I believe so.

I learn, later, that the bank was situated at Kilcreggan in Scotland, that the other boy's name was Keith Nutter and that we were going after blackberries. There seems to have been no adults around, but I suppose they must have been watching despite the road being isolated and our homes not a hundred yards away. I am told that when we returned we had stuffed the blackberries into the pockets of our shorts and the juice had stained us and them. I cannot think my mother was very pleased, but she always laughed when she told the story.

Kilcreggan is on the north shore of the Firth of Clyde, across the water from Gourock, where my father, at that time a Petty Officer in the Royal Navy, was stationed after the war. I have the impression that Gourock is the site of a naval dockyard, but grown-ups didn't tell you much in those days or in the years that followed. A ferry crosses the Clyde between the two places. We must have used the ferry on many occasions.

On the beach at Kilcreggan with Dad, 1947

The homes to which Keith and I returned, our pockets

laden with fruit, were Nissen huts. I remember the curved sheet of corrugated metal and the stable door. Wartime shortages required these homes to be economical in their use of materials, easily portable and speedily erected; they could be packed in a standard Army wagon and built by six men in four hours.

The car is a taxi and the driver performs this manoeuvre often, no doubt to amuse us children, and it does.

It is a time remembered with affection by my parents. Names are repeated like charms: Kilcreggan, Gourock, Helensburgh, Rosneath. They mean nothing to me as I sit listening to the grown-ups but they exude a sense of warmth and homeliness that permeate my early years. I know the time there was enjoyable for me; it was always summer or on the edge of summer, and there was dust and blue skies and the air was warm on my arm. My father later called Scotland 'God's own country'. The photographs show a little boy with his blond hair combed straight; he looks well fed. He is laughing

On the beach at Kilcreggan with Mum, 1947

as he leans against the door of the hut and as he rides a tricycle with his friend.

These must have been the early years of my parents' marriage. Their wedding was in January 1940 and I was born in April 1944. After the war ended in 1945 my father returned home and began settling down to life with his family. He wrote in his private diary:

"I joined (the navy) because working in civil (sic) street is alright when there is work to do but when all this armament programme is over there will naturally be a slump and many good men losing jobs. I want to get married and do the best for my wife and children and by behaving myself I shall have a pension at the end of twenty-two years and a regular job till then."

My mother's National Registration Identity Card records that we lived in RN Married Quarters at Portkill, Kilcreggan from April to October 1947. Later I learn that she did not want to move from married quarters to married quarters wherever my father was stationed. *Was this because she did not like them or because she wanted a stable home for my sister and me?*

The Nissen hut had a central hallway with rooms going off from either side, and I believe there was a large room at the far end, but that is all I can picture: I am unable to enter any of the rooms and see them as they were. A photograph of the site shows me that the huts, about forty in number, were grouped back-to-back and in a circular manner. Ours must have been facing the cornfield, dotted with stooks of wheat or barley, along the foot of which the dusty road must have run. Others face the sea. Washing is hanging from lines strung between the huts. Real houses (those of the locals?) are situated near the edge of the Firth of Clyde.

Other than her holding me as the taxi drew to a halt, I have no memory of my mother at this time – washing me, feeding me, playing with me, reading to me, taking me for walks – but

I know that she did because I remember the stories and the nursery rhymes. One in particular resonates:

> 'Tom, Tom the piper's son
> Stole a pig and away he run
> The pig was eat and Tom was beat
> And Tom went roaring down the street.'

In the picture accompanying the rhyme, a man in a kilt is shaking a gnarled stick at Tom, who is haring towards me with a small pig under his arm. *It is another twenty years or so before I discover that the 'pig' was not an animal at all but more likely to be a small, apple pie.*

Of my father, I have no memory at this time, but I still possess a wooden trolley filled with wooden cubes: all handmade and hand-painted in bold colours – reds and greens and, particularly, yellows. It is on wheels and I must have pulled it along by a piece of string attached to the front. Vaguely, very vaguely, I can remember sitting on it and being pulled. Who the puller was I have no idea, but my father certainly made the trolley and the cubes. Well, cubes they are but we always referred to them as bricks.

The photographs show us on the beach at Kilcreggan. My father is kneeling beside me, smiling, in one; in the other my mother stands behind supporting me. In both, I have my head tilted slightly towards my left shoulder. This stance is repeated in all the photographs: with Keith Nutter on our trikes, leaning on the doorjamb of the Nissen hut and in the arms of my grandad. It is a habit I never lost; to this day, if I catch sight of myself, unawares, my head is tilted to one side. *Was this out of shyness or was I thinking?*

In the photograph with my grandad and grandmother, I am also on the beach but dressed very smartly in a thigh-length coat with a velvet collar, white ankle socks and leather shoes with a cross strap. My grandparents, too, are in their best clothes: my grandad wearing a collar and tie with a blazer and flannels, my grandmother in a two-piece suit over a neat blouse and with a handkerchief in her jacket pocket. These were my mother's parents: George Frederick and Anna-Maria Warden, nee Last, but more of them later.

While we were there King George VI and Queen Elizabeth (later the Queen Mother) inspected the 'Royal Navy on the Clyde' when the home fleet visited in July 1947. They were accompanied by HRH Princess Margaret. A souvenir programme of the event, costing 6d, lists all the ships and their locations. It also contains messages from Viscount Hall, First Lord of the Admiralty, and Sir Hector McNeil, Lord Provost of Glasgow as well as a glossary of naval terms.

My father had served a five-year apprenticeship as a cabinetmaker before signing on for twenty-two years in the Royal Navy and was regarded highly for his craftsmanship. A letter received from his commanding officer soon after we left Kilcreggan confirms this:

> "*I could always be quite certain of placing you in a really first class job in civvy street.*"

An attachment continues:

> "*A communication has been received from the above rating (my father) stating that the entry of his efficiency in his service certificate ... signed by me as Commanding Officer HMS Rosneath could be read as 'sat' or 'supr' ... This rating was well known to me personally and there can be no doubt that his assessment should have been 'supr'.*

My father was obviously not satisfied at being simply 'sat', which I take to mean 'satisfactory': nothing short of 'superb' (or was it 'super' or 'supreme') would do for him. It must have taken considerable nerve writing to his commanding officer questioning the legibility of the man's handwriting.

The letter – on thin, wartime paper – was addressed to 4, Turin Street, Ipswich. I have no recollection of how we travelled to Suffolk – presumably it must have been by train – but Turin Street was to be home during the formative years of my childhood.

Outside the Nissen huts with Keith Nutter on our tricycles, 1947

Chapter Two
The House in Turin Street

Arriving home from Scotland in November 1947, my parents lifted me up and over the concrete step of 4, Turin Street, Ipswich. This step was scrubbed daily to a shining whiteness by my mother; no other front doorstep in the street matched hers for cleanliness. It was a step so unsullied by dirt that stepping over rather than on it was always the preferred option, made impossible by the steep rise from the pavement.

They took me in through the front door, which opened into the front room. Unless I was playing out this was the way I would always come home. Not that we lingered there long: the front room was a sanctuary for all that was treasured and above common daily usage. It was set aside for callers if they were welcome beyond the street, but it was otherwise reserved for very special occasions; even Christmas was careful not to take too great an advantage of its hospitality. Here, the best furniture held pride of place and the best china graced a cabinet: 'best' in the sense that I rarely recall it being used. There was a mirror over the fireplace and china ornaments on the mantelpiece.

Occasionally, if the coast was clear because Mum was at the shops, I would venture into this room. If I was feeling particularly bold, I might dare to lift an ornament from its place; if I did it was always held tightly in both hands. Once, having discovered where the key was hidden, I actually opened the china cabinet but wasn't brave enough to remove a single item. Not only was I fearful of a breakage but also of not returning the piece to its exact position on the glass shelf: my mother seemed to know the precise angle at which her treasured possessions rested.

The door from this sanctum opened into the living room, where there was a place for everything and everything was in its place. A sideboard stood against the right-hand wall; the top drawer contained daily cutlery, the second tableware, the third board games and the lower holiday knick-knacks, photographs in albums or loose in cardboard boxes and oddities my dad brought home from abroad. The cupboard to the right stored crockery and the one to the left held cake stands. In this cupboard my mother kept a chocolate Father Christmas wrapped in gold and red foil, which I refused to eat because it looked so attractive. The cupboards snapped to with spring catches that squeaked. The dining table, where we ate and played board games, held centre stage. The facing wall contained two doors and a sash window: the window opened onto the back yard, the centre door opened onto the stairs and that to the right onto the kitchen. The fireplace with its mottled brown tile surround and mantelpiece, set into the wall opposite the sideboard, was the only source of heat in the house unless a fire was lit in the upstairs rooms, and this never happened, partly because of safety, no doubt, but also because it was not considered necessary. Who needed heat in a bedroom?

The term 'living room' is an apt description: there we lived, ate, played, talked and listened. Here my imagination was first fired. *Was this where I became such a good listener? Yes, I think it started here, cuddled down on the hearthrug.* Alone with my mother – my father initially based at Chatham and my sister yet to be born – I listened to her reading nursery rhymes and stories. Books in those times were printed on rough paper and colour printing was in its infancy, but they enthralled nonetheless. I recall a collection of *Brer Rabbit* tales with a black, red and white cover. These tales were told by Uncle Remus and the cover showed a black man, smiling; his eyes were filled with the humour of his stories.

The most frightening adventures of all were contained within the Rupert books; these were the early Rupert stories written by Mary Tourtel where evil reined and dark magic lurked. Only the little bear's loyalty to his friends and theirs to him saved the day. I remember those stories as vividly now as when my mother – and, surely, my grandad – read them to me by the fireside in Turin Street. The first of these (still on my shelf to this day) has a coloured cover but the illustrations are black and white. Another contains one story in particular – *Rupert, the Witch and Tabitha* – that gave me fruitful and fearful nightmares whenever it came to the dark of the bedroom. Rupert stops on his way home from the market to help an old woman who claims to have sprained her ankle. The little bear helps her through the dark wood to her 'dreary cottage' with its 'bleak and gloomy air' only to be told that his mummy and daddy will never find him because:

> *"He'll never find you", sneered the crone,*
> *Giving him an evil look,*
> *For this is an enchanted wood,*
> *And every step you took*
>
> *Covered seven miles. Now you can count*
> *The steps you took, and so*
> *You'll know how far you are from home,*
> *Hundreds of miles, Ho! Ho!"*

The terror those words struck in me is as alive now as it was nearly seventy years ago: the idea that anyone could be lured hundreds of miles from home and imprisoned with no chance of finding their loved ones again remains horrifying. *There is no harm in nightmarish tales: they prepare a child for the worst possibilities in life.* As I lay awake wondering, I was already planning what I might do to escape; I learned from Rupert that kindness brings its own rewards and to trust your friends. He befriends the old crone's cat, which was lured to her cottage as a kitten, and the cat's knowledge helps them escape together.

In this room, too, my mother and I listened to the radio. The first of these was a small, purple set with white knobs that yellowed with time; it bore the name Marconi and was made of plastic. The second was a larger model made of veneered plywood cut in curves polished to a high shine, and on the front of which a dog listened to a gramophone; the tuning dial moved a needle that made its way across a backlit screen bearing the names of the radio stations.

There was an intensity of concentration when we listened to the radio; although it wasn't necessary, it always seemed to help if you could see the set, if only with the occasional glance. As I remember, it was placed to one side of the fireplace, around which we would sit while listening, and we would either look across to it, in summer, or gaze down into the flames, in winter. Years later, when I came to read *Our Mutual Friend*, I claimed an immediate affinity with Lizzie Hexam and her ability to read the flames:

> "When I look at (the fire) of an evening, it comes like pictures to me, Charley."
> "Show us a picture," said the boy, "Tell us where to look."
> "Ah! It wants my eyes, Charley."
> "Cut away then, and tell us what your eyes make of it."

Listening to words, as distinct from watching pictures, conjures images in the mind. I can see Grace trapped in the burning stable as she attempts to rescue her horses in *The Archers*, Sherlock Holmes in the room at Stoke Moran waiting for the snake to curl its way down the bell rope in *The Speckled Band*, Lemmy lost on the walls of the Martian city in *Journey Into Space*, PC49 taking toffee from the jar and Paul Temple's train leaving the station. It is these adventure series or serials, which always ended on a cliffhanger, that still hold my imagination. Even today, when listening to someone talking my mind creates pictures to accompany the words.

We listened to other shows on the BBC Light Programme or Home Service: *Desert Island Discs*, *Two Way Family Favourites* for the servicemen stationed abroad, *A Life of Bliss* with Percy Edwards barking Psyche the dog, *The Billy Cotton Band Show* introduced by that dreadful shout of 'Wakey! Wakey!' *Children's Hour* with Jennings and Darbishire, *Educating Archie* and its string of comic talent including Max Bygraves, Beryl Reid, Benny Hill, Dick Emery, Sid James and James Robertson Justice, *Hancock's Half Hour* set at Railway Cuttings in East Cheam, *Have a Go* with 'Mabel at the table' and 'Harry Hudson at the piano', *Listen with Mother* that would begin when we were 'sitting comfortably', *Record Roundup* with Jack Jackson interspersing the records with monologues by popular, often American, comedians, *The Navy Lark* with its catch phrase, "Left hand down a bit", addressed to the helmsman, *Take It From Here* and the Glums with June Whitfield's long sigh "Oh Ron ..." and Dick Bentley's dim-witted reply "Yes, Eth" and *Worker's Playtime* with an impressionist called Peter Goodwright.

There must have been many more, but these live in my personal memory; and what I remember about these shows are the distinctive voices of the characters and the signature tunes. They filled our living room, and I can still picture the places; the workers' canteens, Ron and Eth's living room. Why can I recall such things from fifty or sixty years ago and, perhaps even more strangely, see them?

Board games were played on the table: ludo, snakes and ladders, Chinese chequers, tiddly-winks and draughts. The game was only part of the pleasure: it was the company and the conversation that lingered in the mind. We learned about each other during those games: who must win, who could lose with their dignity intact.

My father, always home at the weekends when stationed at Chatham and every evening once stationed at Shotley, taught a mean version of ludo called 'hukkers': this was the Navy's take on the children's game, and he must have played it in the mess on many occasions. It was designed for two players, each with two of the colours, but could be played less frenetically by four. It involved 'blobbing up', 'attacking your blob' and 'mixed blobs'; a blob was two or more of a player's colour on top of each other, and no other player could pass the blob unless, from a position directly behind it, they attacked the blob by shaking the requisite number of sixes – one for each counter. This was a risky manoeuvre, but if it paid off all the opposing players counters were returned to base, which meant they must start their run again. A defiant blob could hold up the other players and, since they must move if the number on the dice enabled a move, it could also force them into building a mixed blob behind. Since a mixed blob could be wiped out if another player simply landed on it by throwing the correct number, a player could find all their counters returned to base. The strategist blobbed up on the way as often as possible and the brave strategist blobbed up at the top of their home run. It was considered cowardly to run for home; holding on to that final blob was the mark of a man.

 I have said there was no heating in the house except the fire in this room, and it was round this fire that we crowded during the winter months. There was something primitive, reminiscent of Neanderthal man huddled round wood fires in the mouth of the cave, about the central role of this fire in our lives during the cold season – something primitive and pleasant. I can smell the crumpets toasting and hear the sound of my mother's knitting needles as we gaze into the flames; I can hear the spit of chestnuts and feel the heat on my hands as I retrieve them from the scuttle. We sat, night after night, huddled in front of the coal fire, our faces burning with the heat and our backs as cold as ice. The house was draughty, and external doors were hung with curtains and blocked with draught excluders, but the cold on our backs was intensified by the contrast; the heat from the coals did not travel far into the room, let alone elsewhere in the house. Everyone was reluctant to make a move to bed.

In the backyard at Turin Street, circa 1949

The stairs led from the living room through the central door and wound their way, initially, to two rooms upstairs. I think mine was the first room, and that my parents had to pass through it to reach theirs, because I can recall lying in bed watching the window that opened onto the back yard. In winter, this window would ice over on the inside:

> *Look out, look out, Jack Frost is about*
> *He's after your fingers and toes*
> *And all through the night, that gay little sprite*
> *Is working when nobody knows*
> *He'll climb each tree, so nimble is he*
> *And his silvery powder he'll shake*
> *And while we're asleep*
> *To our windows he'll creep*
> *And such beautiful patterns he'll make.*

It was true. The morning light shining through the window lit his patterns to perfection; it was just a shame that our breath condensed in the air as we lay in bed. Mum always allowed us to get ready for bed downstairs in front of the fire. It was a matter of absorbing the available heat and then making a dash up the stairs. There was, of course, the hot water bottle – rubber or stone – and this heated a small portion of the bed. Too hot to be touched by your feet it was usually pushed to the bottom of the bed, although on very cold nights I would hug it close. As the bed warmed from your body heat, a tentative foot and then a hand would make their way outwards until they reached the Frigid Zone; in this way, it was possible to trace the shape of one's body in the confines of the bed. The warmth never spread far. We always had sheets and blankets and these were stretched tight and tucked in firmly – tucked in so firmly that it was always a struggle to get out of bed in the morning.

Later, I was to move to a third upstairs room. This appeared suddenly sometime after my sister was born, and I can only think that my father must have had it built as an extension. This third bedroom was located over the kitchen and the window looked out over the roofs of the toilet and coal shed. By then my listening had matured into reading and with Enid Blyton's *Secret Seven* I had many an adventure, some of which involved my leaving the house quietly over the roof of the outhouses. Just as I had walked with the Wise Old Goat and taken on the Old Man of the Sea and many a vicious crone with Rupert, I now joined the Secret Seven on more domestic – and, possibly, more realistic – adventures. Her children peopled my room alongside Dan Dare, Biggles and, later still, Bulldog Drummond. I never liked the Famous Five, finding them to be utterly snobbish: working class people like my family and me were always dirty to them, and likely to be crooks. Besides, I was suspicious of a girl called George, just as I had been puzzled why Paul Temple's wife had a man's name – Steve. *Were early prejudices forming?*

Below my second bedroom was the kitchen. Reached from the third door off the living room, it boasted a further two doors: one led to the back yard and the other to the pantry.

The pantry was a narrow room with a meat safe and a cold slab. Fridges had yet to be introduced into our country and the cold slab was vital in keeping butter from melting in summer and milk cool all year. The milk was usually placed in a bowl of cold water as an extra precaution against it going sour. Slabs of a cooking fat called Lard, in its white wrapping with the red writing, were always present. The meat safe was a small, wooden box with a wire mesh front. The wooden shelves above the slab contained, among Mum's food store, the bottles of orange juice and cod-liver oil issued by the government to keep us children healthy; the orange juice I loved, but the unused bottles of cod-liver oil steadily increased in number. I remember, too, packets of Farley's rusks; these had a particularly nourishing taste when dunked in tea or softened with warm milk. We were never allowed in the pantry and we never helped ourselves to food. Rationing and war shortages had made mother cautious, and she was always on our tail if she heard the door open.

The kitchen also contained the only sink in the house under which was stored a packet of Omo washing powder and a tube of a coarse powder called Ajax that Mum used to scour everything in sight.

But above all else this sink was where we strip-washed every day, drawing water from the one cold-water tap. The ritual of ear scrubbing – as only mothers of that generation could scrub ears – has never left me. To this day, I shower every morning. The strip wash, which I practised right through my first year at teacher training college because there were no showers or baths there either, was an art form and a ritual. It was necessary to heat the water in a kettle, and for the expert one kettle full would suffice. Standing on a small towel placed over a mat on the concrete kitchen floor, you stripped completely naked. Soap and a flannel were provided. Washing began with the face and progressed down the body, although washing the legs preceded that of the buttocks and anal region. The tricky bit was to get in between the toes, otherwise mother would oblige when she came to check that you were clean. The art was to use enough soap to clear any possibility of dirt but not to allow the hot water in the bowl to become too soapy; if you did, then the only way to rinse the soap from your body was with cold water from the tap. Strip-washing was accomplished with speed because the water in the bowl, especially during the winter months, cooled very rapidly.

The kitchen also contained the cooker, the copper and the Acme wringer, which replaced the old-fashioned mangle.

The copper came into its own on Monday, which was washday, and on bath night, which was Friday. It was a metal tub, heated by an element sited in the base. Cold water was poured into the top from a bucket and let out using a tap into another bucket, which was then emptied into the bath.

On washday, teeth clicking furiously, my mother would wash clothes, sheets, nappies, towels and whatever was soiled, whatever the weather. These would be hung on the line that stretched from the house to a pole at the end of the garden; a clothes prop lifted the middle of the line once Mum had hauled it up on a pulley. The traditional Somerset song sums up, beautifully, the ritual of a woman's domestic duties in the 1950s:

> *'Twas on a Monday morning*
> *When I beheld my darling*
> *She looked so neat and charming*
> *In ev'ry high degree*
> *She looked so neat and nimble, O*
> *A-washing of her linen, O*
> *Dashing away with the smoothing iron*
> *Dashing away with the smoothing iron*
> *She stole my heart away.*

On Tuesday we find the housewife *'a-hanging out her linen, O'*; on Wednesday, she is *'a-starching of her linen, O'*; on Thursday, she is *'a-ironing of her linen, O'*; on Friday, she is *'a-folding of her linen, O'*; on Saturday she is *'a-airing of her linen, O'*; on Sunday, she is *'a-wearing of her linen, O'*. The order and ritual had to be maintained so that everyone had clothes to wear, clean sheets on their bed, nappies on bottoms and towels to wipe themselves dry after the daily strip-wash. It was a hard life. In the winter months in particular, airing was a real bind as the family and the clothes horse fought for a place in front of the fire. My mother's sympathies were divided between keeping us warm and airing the clothes. Scorching the clothes was the great horror. The intense heat of the fire would often scorch the clothes of the unwary housewife; she was always on her guard against this mishap and the request to an older me to, "keep an eye on the clothes while I pop to the shops" was a nightmare in the offing.

My memory of the cooker is less exact: I have a vague image of something speckled blue with white doors, and gas comes to mind; but this must be wrong because it is unaccompanied by that dreadful smell. (My sister tells me that, "Mum hated gas and always had an electric cooker".)

Of what came from the cooker, however, I have a very clear memory. Despite food rationing, which lasted until I was ten in 1954, we ate well. Part of the reason for this was probably my grandad's allotment, but mainly it rested in the cookery skills of my mother. Sunday was always a roast dinner with roast potatoes, three types of vegetable from those in season, Suffolk-style Yorkshire puddings (small and cooked individually in a baking tin), lashings of rich gravy and whatever meat was obtainable on the ration that week; this left enough meat for Monday and Tuesday when we might eat it cold with bubble and squeak (the greens and potato left over from Sunday) or Mum might make a meat pie or a stew or a casserole plumped out with plenty of root vegetables. Friday was invariably a day for fish and chips, while on the other days we had liver and bacon, toad-in-the-hole or sausage and mash; these meat dishes were always, but always, enhanced by the quality of the gravy, which was rich and wholesome enough to stand by you for the rest of the day. Liver – an offal and probably cheap – was a great favourite of mine. Mum dusted it with flour before frying, and it was served crisp and tangy with a small amount of bacon. Quite often Spam was offered, straight or battered, and I loved Spam. I enjoyed opening the tin with the little key attached to the side, and I was quite happy to have it in sandwiches on a picnic.

We ate three square meals a day, and no quarter was given. We were brought up to clear our plates and we cleared our plates. "Eat up your greens. They're good for you" wasn't an encouragement: it was a command. We were given what was considered good for us rather than what we liked. No alternatives were offered because there were no alternatives: apart from the ration, money was short. *Years later, I reared my own children according to the same dictum.* There was no savagery in this attitude, no suggestion that my mother was unfeeling towards our likes and dislikes: just an insistence. The one food I couldn't tolerate was tomatoes and Mum never obliged me to eat them, but an aunt cured me of this in 1951 when I stayed with her while Mum was giving birth to my sister, Linda.

Summer was a wonderful time for eating because Mum served salads, often accompanied by corned beef, another favourite. Lashings of salad cream curling from the bottle added zest to an already delicious array of flavours. Mum created her salads in a bowl, layering the lettuce, cucumber, spring onions, radishes and sliced tomatoes from the bottom to the top. I even liked tomatoes served with a salad. All of this food was free, of course, by virtue of Grandad's work on his allotment.

Our three square meals were breakfast, lunch (called dinner) around noon and tea. Tea was served at 4 o'clock and was the last meal of the day for us children. It was often referred to as 'high tea' because it usually involved a small cooked meal. My favourite among these was Mum's version of Welsh rabbit. *(Don't tell me it's 'rarebit'! The correct title is 'rabbit', and those who spell it otherwise should be ashamed of themselves. If anyone doubts this, check the origins of the dish.)* Mum produced her version by blending the cheese with egg and tomatoes *(perhaps it was her way of getting me to eat them before my aunt intervened?)* and, undoubtedly, the tomatoes added a tang to the dish; it was served on warm, buttered toast and I loved it.

With dinner, Mum also served a dessert, which we called 'afters', and these were always a winner. Rice pudding with a spoonful of jam, spotted dick with custard made from Bird's Custard Powder, jam roly-poly pudding, bread and butter pudding (a great favourite of mine) to use up any stale bread, tinned fruit with Carnation milk or pink blancmange, apple pies in season and to accompany any of these dishes the luxury of Neapolitan ice-cream. *To her dying day, my mother always found room for ice-cream and once cleared, by herself, a bowl of toffee-flavoured ice cream, fruit, syrup, cream and profiteroles that had been designed for two to share!*

We rarely snacked; it was not encouraged and there were few snack foods to buy in the shops. Occasionally, however, if we arrived home hungry, Mum would give us a slice of bread and beef dripping (which was unspeakably delicious), bread coated with sugar or bread and jam.

Both bread and potatoes played a huge part in our diet. Whatever the meal, there was always a plate of bread and butter on the table to fill us up. At teatime, the aunt who cured me of my tomato aversion insisted, if I wanted a second cake, that I had another slice of bread first.

The back door always seemed too high for me to be able to reach the latch, but I must have been able to do so eventually because of one very basic need. A four-foot wide strip of concrete led to two outhouses attached to the house: the first of these was the coal-shed, where we also hung the tin bath, and the other was the toilet.

Yes, the toilet is an outdoor one: hence the need to master that latch. The alternative would be to use the chamber pot placed under every bed for use at night, but I never liked to pee in the pot, let alone do a number two. The idea that my mother would have to empty the pots in the morning, I found revolting. I forget how I mastered the height of the back door and its latch – perhaps it was just age and growing taller – but I did; many a cold night, I'd make my way from bed to the outdoor toilet, where everything was flushed away by pulling the chain attached to the cistern high above the seat.

It has since become a joke that people either kept coal in their bath (northerners) or kept the bath in the coal shed (southerners) but there was nowhere else they could be stored. Every Friday night my mother would fill the copper with water and heat it up. At first, the small, oval bath and, later, the long one would be collected from its nail on the coal shed wall and wiped clean. It would then be filled from the tap on the copper, which would be refilled. Hot water was difficult to produce and, therefore, at a premium, and so my sister and I shared the bathwater: she first and then me. I complained but my father was quite clear on the matter:

"Your sister is a lady and, therefore, comes first. Besides you should be pleased to bath in a maiden's widdle."

I wasn't really convinced, but was this where my sense of chivalry was born? I still open doors for women and if there's only milk for one cup of tea, my wife has that cup.

Behind the toilet – overlooking the rest of this so-small garden – was an open, covered place where the dustbins and garden tools were stored. In front of this were two wooden tubs of flowers and the small patch between the end of the outhouses and the back fence. This was a lawn at one time, bordered with my mother's flowers, but what I really remember is the shed my father built on that spot, where he did his carpentry and I stood drawing in the smell of so many different woods. The shavings fell to the floor and they, too, had a special aroma and curled wonderfully all by themselves. *Was this where I developed my love of wood and wooden objects?*

My father had lighting in his workshop. I think I'm sure of this because I can picture flexes and plugs and I know he used a few electrically operated tools. But this is a puzzle because there was no lighting in the outside toilet as I recall (there, we fumbled in the dark) and there was no lighting in the coal shed, which made life difficult when going out for a late night hod of coal. The workshop came late in our days at Turin Street, I think, and so, perhaps, it was the most modern part of the house. The floor was wooden planks as distinct from the lino in the house: green, canvas-backed lino that curled in the corners. *Is this where I came to hate lino and love carpets!*

This was the house in Turin Street where I spent my childhood. The street was two rows of terraced houses, about twenty on either side. At the rear they bordered on a back alley that separated their gardens from those of Pauline Street, an identical street further on. The alley was 'paved' with the type of black grit similar to that used on what were called 'hard surface' tennis courts: hard they were, and it was best not to fall or you would arrive home your knee embedded with grit.

Linda's christening. From the left, Grandad and Nana Bathstreet, Grandad and Nana Westerfield, Dad, Beattie Barber, 1951

Chapter 3
Mother and Father

Mum and Dad met at Tibbenham's in Ipswich; she was training as an upholstress and he was serving a five-year apprenticeship as a furniture restorer and cabinetmaker. They were both destined to be skilful craftspeople: he in wood and she in fabric. Tibbenham's was a company that specialised in high-quality reproduction furniture, particularly in the Jacobean and Tudor styles. They were also involved in furniture restoration. Their workshops were situated in Turret Lane.

Dad had wanted to join the Royal Navy when he was sixteen but his mother had objected. He wrote in his private diary:

"I joined the Navy in March 1939 because since I was sixteen it has been one of my ambitions ... Naturally my mother didn't want me to leave home ... I waited until I was twenty-one and then of course I had been apprenticed for five years as a reproduction chair and cabinet maker ..."

Their courtship photographs show an immaculately dressed couple: he in suit and tie or Oxford bags and what these days would be called a tank top, she in calf-length skirt and blouse or a two-piece suit. Whether boating, enjoying the park with a friend's dog or relaxing on the beach, their attire remains more or less the same.

Their marriage took place on 27 January 1940 at St Mary at Stoke Church with the reception at the Loco Men's Hut in Rectory Road: Mum's father was a railwayman.

Dad told me many years later that he had been in no hurry to get married at that particular time because he wanted to make a significant contribution to the war effort that might have involved the obvious risk.

Mum and Dad with Aunty Betty and her brother, Curly, who was Dad's best man, pre 1939

My mother was a bride of the war years and a woman of her time. Hers was the last generation of women to view the title 'wife and mother' as a full-time commitment. During the 1950s, many women had to work, at least part-time, to supplement the income of their husbands, but this was not the case for my mother. She chose to stay at home and raise her children and was proud to do so; she saw her role as being not only a duty but also vitally important. Whether or not she might have wanted to continue working after she was married was never an issue. Certainly, her kind of work was there and certainly it would have boosted the household income, but she saw her role as that of wife and mother; it was not a role she considered to be in any way demeaning.

There was a cosy feel to our home, and my mother was responsible for this feeling of security from which we benefitted. Mum was always at hand and we were grateful for her presence, especially in times of illness, and there were many of those.

As a housewife, she had a significant daily workload. I've already mentioned washdays and bath nights: both huge undertakings in the conditions prevalent at the time. In addition, it was her task to 'make ends meet', shop each day for groceries because they had to be bought in small amounts, ensure that three wholesome meals a day were provided for the family and cooked from fresh produce, repair and alter old clothes, sew or knit new ones, keep the house healthily clean and then, of course, there was baking day.

Besides these demands on her time, there were the children: me from 1944 and my sister, Linda, from 1951. We were on her hands all day for the greater part of eleven years. My father worked many miles away: even when he moved to *HMS Ganges* at Shotley it was a twelve mile bike ride each way. The only telephones were those on street corners, and a phone call would only be made in a real emergency. Mother, then, was fully responsible (and, by definition, fully culpable) and on her own; she was, in every sense of the word, the key decision-maker where we children were concerned. It must have seemed, at times, to be an awesome trust.

And it was a trust: the natural bond that exists between mother and child was strengthened immeasurably by her obligations to us during that time in our lives.

We were often sick – subject to ailments from which all children of the 50s suffered: chicken pox, measles, German measles, tonsillitis, mumps and whooping cough. I managed to avoid the latter two, leaving my mother worried that I might contract mumps as an adult and become sterile, but I succumbed to the rest badly and also developed rheumatic fever, which obliged my mother to carry me round on a cushion for a number of months. I also contracted yellow jaundice, which has meant that I have never been welcome at blood banks. My rude health as an adult (I only ever had one week off work because of illness in forty years) must be down to her expert mothering when I was a child. Mother and nurse: Mum fulfilled both roles admirably.

Despite the undoubted quality of her care when it was really needed, she was not one to make or appreciate any fuss over what she termed 'minor ailments' or 'general aches and pains'. Where they were concerned, we were expected to 'get on with it', along with the rest of the children on the street. Three general cures high on her list were Syrup of Figs, Milk of Magnesia and Andrews Liver Salts. I quite enjoyed the latter once the fizzing had stopped but tried to avoid the others like the plague. I was never sure what complaints any of these patent medicines would remedy, but I do remember my mother's obsession with 'wind' and my father's belief in 'a good huck out'; *it may or may not be a testament to them that I have never experienced any problems with my intestinal tract as an adult.*

Other treatments included a lotion called White Horse Embrocation, which Mum rubbed into any area that was giving us pain (I remember its rather pungent smell) and for colds, flu and the sniffles your towel-covered head was placed over a bowl of hot water containing Vick. When you finally emerged a spoonful of Rosehip Syrup was placed in your mouth.

Visits to the doctor had not been an option prior to the establishment of the National Health Service, but by the 1950s they were ready to make house calls. Our local doctor lived quite close, his house and front garden opening onto Wherstead Road, and during my many ailments I can recall his presence in the house: striped suit, sleek-backed hair, large hands and brown medical bag. He would lean over attentively, take my temperature, feel my pulse and recommend that Mum "carried on with the treatment" and kept me "in the warm".

'In the warm' was a high priority when you were ill; there was no wrapping you up and bundling you off to school because Mum was there to look after you. I can feel the warmth of the bed with the blankets and sheets pulled high up on my neck, being spoon fed with egg custard or bread in warm milk to 'build up your strength', bottles of Lucozade, which was an expensive luxury, and being able to sleep:

> *'Sleep that knits up the ravelled sleeve of care*
> *The death of each day's life, sore labour's bath*
> *Balm of hurt minds, great nature's second course*
> *Chief nourisher in life's feast'*

Never was a truer word spoken: when you are ill, sleep is the great nourisher.

The three great fears in those days were scarlet fever, polio and tuberculosis. I never came across the first (except when I contracted a mild form on teaching practice) but the sight of children with one leg fastened in callipers was common enough to be distressing and the fear with TB was that you would be incarcerated in a sanatorium, where 'even your parents wouldn't be allowed to visit you'. *How true this was I do not know, but it was the stuff of nightmares at the time.*

Mum was apt to ignore sickness in herself. I only knew her take to bed on one occasion, when Dad had to look after us and was at a loss as to how he might boil an egg. I put this down to attitude rather than robust health: she was of a generation of women who simply couldn't afford to be sick because so much and so many depended on them. It was a form of stubbornness, and Mum was stubborn. This manifested itself in several ways: some amusing and others not so amusing. Stubbornness at times bordered on the recalcitrant. Once her mind was made up there was no changing her opinion or her decision on any action she intended to take. She wouldn't disagree with you, but sit silently absorbing what you might have to say and when you finished state, quite simply: "Yes, dear."

I felt, at times, that the calmness was as much a force of circumstances as it was her nature. I can only make assumptions concerning its origin. I suppose it must have infuriated Dad, but he never showed any frustration. Later in life, she accomplished a complete turn-around.

"What do you think, dear?" she would ask when decisions needed to be made.

She had a temper on her, and perhaps it was this that her stubbornness was keeping under control. This temper worked for and against us.

I recall one occasion when the father of another boy had pursued me along the passageway. I forget what I had done. His son was one of those children who are always on the edge of friendship, but are never really accepted by the group. Perhaps I had upset him. Whatever the reason, his father pursued me to our back gate, which I must have shut between us. An altercation then broke out with my mother who seized a yard broom and chased the man back along the passage. She must have been in the middle of her housework and dressed for the occasion because I'll never forget the sight of her – scarf on head with the little front knot blowing in the rush, apron flapping and yard broom raised aloft – harrowing this man to his own yard. She seemed quite invigorated on her return and never questioned me about what I might have said or done; it was quite enough for her that someone had threatened her child.

On the other hand, my sister and I sometimes felt the lash of her anger ourselves; for Linda it came with a slap on the legs and for me with a slap round the head. On one occasion, I had persuaded Mum to let me go out and play after I had been dressed smartly for a weekend visit to Dad's family at Westerfield.

"If I let you go out," she urged, "don't go and get yourself messed up."

Unfortunately I did just that and returned with a smudge on the collar of my fresh, white polo shirt. The shirt was removed, cleaned and replaced; and my ear stung with the blow.

It is easy, nowadays – when a child being slapped is seen as verging almost on the sadistic and is certainly viewed as inexcusable and heartless – to condemn such an action. But life is easier, now, softer: no woman faces washday as the hard work of a whole week. And, no, I did not grow up to slap my own children. I was learning to be a father even then, and one way we learn is through the mistakes of others.

It was almost certainly in the same headstrong state of mind that Mum insisted on having all her teeth removed. I think this happened before my time, but I am unsure. Mum had fallen from her bike and broken, severely, her front teeth. The state of the damage was such that they needed to be removed. When the dentist, who would have been paid privately if the accident occurred prior to the establishment of the NHS, came to undertake the task, Mum said: "All or none."

Despite not being present, I can hear her saying it. It wouldn't happen today; the dentist would refuse to oblige. Back then, he extracted the lot and Mum lived the rest of her life with false teeth, top and bottom. The sight of her dropping these nightly into a glass of Steradent remains with me to this day. (My sister informs me that this memory is inaccurate, that Mum actually kept six of her front bottom teeth to 'give her extra bite'. She remembers coming home from secondary school one day to find Mum 'sitting at the table in obvious discomfort with a scarf around her neck and mouth'.

For Linda and for me, however, Mum's false teeth held one huge advantage. Whenever things were getting on top of her and she was becoming agitated – and Mum agitated was a sight to behold – her teeth would click. This was our four-minute warning to seek shelter – and we did. One learns to read the signs: *another of life's lessons engendered in childhood.*

Growing up, she had been one of three sisters with two younger brothers and you realised this in her manner. They had been a happy family and the girls must have held sway in the home. You can see this in the photographs of that time and we experienced it in the comradeship that existed between them as young married women. There was a briskness about the Warden girls that amused us children; between them they had nine children and we spent much of our childhoods with our cousins. Mum's manner showed the confidence of a woman who had been, and was, part of a large family. When the women were together there was always a shared joke between them, one that no one else understood and went back years but one that lit up the occasion. Each of them had what was called a dirty laugh; it was, in effect, jolly and carefree.

In company, Mum knew her own mind and was outspoken but never vindictive. Soon after Linda was born and we were with Dad's family at Westerfield, the time came for my sister's feed. All of us were gathered round in the living room, and Mum whipped out her breast and started the feed. My grandmother was shocked.

"My God, Edna!" she exclaimed.

Mum never battered an eyelid and went on with the feed. Given the fuss that is now being made, sixty-four years on, about women breastfeeding in public, Mum's action must have been of revolutionary proportions in that little Suffolk village. She was wearing a summer frock at the time and it wasn't designed like today's garments to hide the breast. I remember being both startled (I'd never seen a woman's breast before) and proud.

Looking back, I think that was one of those moments that made me the maverick headteacher I became: never mind the crowd's opinion, just do what you consider to be right. Later, I was to realise that the view of the crowd is almost certain to be wrong simply because it is unconsidered by the individuals within it. Am I my mother's son?

Mum was a snob, I think. Not in the coarse sense in that she looked down on people because of their social status, but in that she thought certain things were proper to one's own position. Certainly, my Uncle Horace thought so, and I think it had been discussed at Westerfield. Horace was married to my Auntie Barbara, Dad's half-sister, and he was a familiar sight when we visited. He once said to me:

"Of course, we all feel your mum is a bit of a snob, Terry. She thinks she's a bit above us."

She may have assumed an aloofness in her relationship with Dad's family, but she never passed any derogatory comments in my hearing. Undoubtedly, there was a degree of uprightness about her, and this might have stemmed from her family. The Wardens were always impeccably dressed. Given the shortages of the 1940s and 50s, it is impressive how smart they all looked. It is clear from snapshots that my maternal grandparents were particular about the way they looked when walking out. They held strong opinions about things being done in the correct manner, but this was a general view of the time.

When we moved from Turin Street in 1957, I do remember Mum saying to me that she – a Labour voter until that time – thought it now appropriate to vote Liberal. Not Conservative, note, which was the province of the moneyed classes, but Liberal: above the working but below the upper class! Also, she always spoke with pride about my being born in Allington House. This was a nursing home on the Woodbridge Road, and the implication was that it was superior in some way to a hospital. Judging from the photographs, Dad was on active service at the time and I rather think that either Mum or her parents may have organised this place for her confinement.

Mum had few interests outside the home, and looking at her working week this is hardly surprising, but she had several connected with her role as wife and mother.

One of these was rug making. She would purchase a base – made, I think, of hessian – and acquire inordinate amounts of wool. These may have been from a rug-making kit or from her previous workmates: about that I am not sure. The wool, which was round in shape, had to be cut into small pieces using a plastic device turned with a handle. Either the pattern for the rug was already marked on the hessian or Mum devised it: whatever the case, we then took the small pieces of wool and, using a needle-like object with a large eye, we inserted the wool through the holes in the hessian and pulled it tight. Many colours were involved and hours of labour. We worked on the living room table and I loved being there with my mother. It was an experience that was absolutely relaxing.

Another of her interests, perhaps out of necessity, was knitting. Again I was involved. No one else could touch my prowess at helping my mother wind the wool into a ball. It came in skeins, which I would hold upon my open, outstretched hands. Mum would then take one end of the skein and while I manoeuvred my hands in a subtle, swaying movement she would wind the wool into a ball. From these endeavours emerged pullovers, sweaters, short-sleeved pullovers, cardigans, socks, and swimming trunks. The trunks are best forgotten. I was not the only child of the fifties to suffer from knitted trunks, but the experience remains very personal, nonetheless: they itched, they fell and the colour ran down your thighs. They were made by your mum, it is true, but the bought ones – once there were ones to buy – were much more comfortable.

Mum's skill at sewing was also appreciated, although whether my sister felt this I am not sure because she wore the dresses. Homemade is all the rage now – at least in principle if not in practice – but in the 50s it could be on sufferance. My mother was extremely skilful at the art of dressmaking. I can see the patterns from which she worked lying on the table as she pours over them, a needle and thread held in her lips, a pair of dressmaking scissors in her right hand. Wedding dresses were often homemade, school dresses always, shirts sometimes and costumes for school plays were no problem at all. She met the challenge of turning one into a cook or a king with equal aplomb. Her machine needed lifting onto the living room table (it was only later Mum obtained a model that folded into its own). I watched her threading the bobbin, open-mouthed in wonder.

She was also a skilled, if untrained, photographer: the snapshots of the time are beautifully composed. With her usual attention to detail she dated every one. All were taken with a Kodak Box Brownie camera.

She also upholstered furniture such as stools made by my father and I rest my feet on one of these even today. *One way in which we live on is in the creations we leave behind us when we go.*

Baking was a weekly business – always cakes and sometimes bread in the oven – and thus birthday baking was a natural outcome of this weekly endeavour. *Watching one of today's 'domestic goddesses' parading a cake they have made on Facebook is both a sad and chastening experience when your memory goes back to those days.* Syrup sponges, carrot cakes, upside-down cakes, angel cakes, Swiss rolls, apple cakes, chocolate sponges, muffins made from fruit in season, Suffolk scones, parkin, flapjacks and (best of all) Battenberg cake rolled from the oven ready for the party – although not all on one occasion! Topping these was the birthday cake itself: always fruit and sometimes with nuts, resplendent with marzipan and iced with the interest of the moment – Rupert Bear or Dan Dare's spaceship. As a boy, I never wondered how Mum found the time in such a busy week or where she found the ingredients; but my friends and I were appreciative as we gathered round the table in our living room.

Rationing was indisputably a real bind for the woman of the day. Mum managed because she had no choice and she was resourceful. She learned to make do and mend. Mum queued regularly for whatever was needed up until 1954. The time involved was lengthened by the fact that the shopping was not confined to one place: beef and pork were sold by two separate butchers, greengrocery could be bought in one shop while actual groceries were available further along the Wherstead Road. If Mum required other household items – such as fabric or thread, kindling and matches or paraffin for Dad's Tilley lamp – she would have to go to the ironmongers!

Her ration book was registered with our local stores, and the store was given only enough food for the people on its list, which ensured that everybody got a fair share, protected the poor from high prices and prevented hoarding. One person's weekly ration was four ounces of lard or butter, 12 ounces of sugar, four ounces of bacon, two eggs, six ounces of meat and two ounces of tea: although these amounts varied according to availability.

We children were more or less unaware of this, but sometimes Mum sent me to Parkers, a grocery store that was on the large side for its day. I had an angelic face at the time topped with blond hair that was brushed and Brylcreemed daily: perhaps she thought my appearance might charm the shopkeeper to exceed the ration allowance! I remember a long, wooden counter curving towards the back of the shop and Mr Parker in his sandy-coloured overall smiling down at me as I held out the ration book. On the counter was a set of black scales with brass weights. Behind the shopkeeper on the shelves were tinned and packet foods and to one side wooden cases of fruit and vegetables. I don't remember there being a great deal of these items but they were available for those who could afford them.

How Mum fed us so well I have no idea – meat, in particular, would have been difficult to obtain beyond the ration – but I cannot imagine that either she or Dad would have approved of the black market. We were, of course, relatively well off because of Dad's forethought in signing on in the Royal Navy for twenty-two years. He had a regular wage, whereas many men were looking for work after the war.

Mother was the key parent, and that must have been sad for my father. I know that at times he felt he was on the sideline.

"I am your father, you know, not just the man who comes home at weekends to do the gardening," he once said as he left on a Sunday night to return to Portsmouth.

Years later, I often heard his voice saying that when I was playing with my own children. I was lucky: teaching allowed me to spend as much time with my children as did their mother. For men of my father's generation, however – and for many men today – travelling in order to find work was, and is, an absolute necessity. Someone in a marriage has to bring the rabbit home for the other to prepare dinner.

Bringing home the proverbial rabbit was a big consideration for men of Dad's generation. Mum told me that when they married he gave her a choice regarding work.

"You can carry on working if you want to," he said, "but if you do I'll give you nothing towards the housekeeping."

He intended to carry on being fully responsible for the household bills (mortgage, insurance, gas and electricity, water, rates and so on) but she would be paying for the food and other daily items. This was not, of course, intended as a suggestion that they should share the costs of marriage as couples do nowadays. He was making it clear that, as a man, he expected to meet all the costs and that Mum should fulfil the roles of wife and mother. There was a huge pride in his kind of man that it was their duty to provide, financially, for the family.

His position was, of course, particularly difficult. He was serving in the Royal Navy and went where he was commanded to go; and mother never took to the idea of living in married quarters, when he was shore based, so that she could be with him.

Initially, following the return from Scotland, he was stationed at Chatham. This was followed by a period when he was stationed at *HMS Ganges*, Shotley, which is about twelve miles from where we lived in Ipswich. It was long bike ride, an hour each way at the beginning and end of each working day, and I can remember him setting off on his BSA pedal cycle with its derailleur gears and drop handlebars. I once asked him what BSA meant.

"Bloody sore arse!" he replied.

These are the years when he was at home each evening. He was happy at that time because he could see himself as a father and husband. He turned a number of items on his lathe – sets of bowls, small barrels with lids to hold buttons and similar objects – for family and friends. He made toys for us: the brick tray, a sword and shield, a wooden horse. For the home he made sets of tables, stools, dining chairs and a number of cabinets both small and large and a clothes horse. His toolboxes – I still have one of these – were works of art, beautifully and lovingly crafted. Dad was a skilled craftsman in an age when this was respected. Like all individual craftsmen, Dad did the complete job: he selected the wood, measured and cut and planed it, jointed and assembled the parts and French polished the complete article, and fixed the handles, locks and shields.

He was a perfectionist, and this was one of his flaws. It was never a question for him of doing the best possible job under the circumstances: each job had to be perfect, and he carried this attitude into his personal life.

One thing I dreaded above all was bringing home my school report.

"Show it to your father, dear," Mum would say.

I stood before him as he pored over each subject on the list with its one-word comments and percentages.

"Why did you only get 69% for comprehension?" he would ask, "Why not 70%?"

That extra percent would have rounded off the numbers for him, but how could a child answer such a question. The obvious reply was, "Ask the teacher. She did the marking." But that would have smacked of cheek, and cheek was not an option for a child in the fifties. Not that Dad ever hit us, but there was an element of fear in the relationship. He would continue down the list in this way, asking unanswerable questions. Never once did I hear "Well done."

"You should be able to take constructive criticism," he would say, "That's the only way we can improve ourselves."

But it wasn't, and isn't. I never forget facing Dad with my school reports, waiting to be belittled. No matter how well

I might have done, I could always do better; and so I grew up feeling inadequate.

But the belittling had its benefits if only for my children and the children I taught. I learnt that a simple "Well done" or a supportive pat on the back if a child was struggling with a concept was worth one hundred thousand constructive criticisms. You don't have to be told you're a brilliant mathematician or given a badge declaring you to be a great gymnast – no child needs or believes such nonsense – but feeling successful breeds further success.

It wasn't until I'd shaken off those years and learned that few things are ever perfect and that one can only do one's best in any endeavour that I learned to appreciate what skills and qualities I might possess.

It was a lesson Dad never learned. The psychology of why I will leave to the textbooks. His father

'was killed in action in the 4th Royal Fusiliers in 1916'

His mother re-married. Dad's stepfather, Harry Davey, was

'the finest stepfather a stepson could have, he has always shown me every consideration and would do anything for me that was in his power and means (a perfect gentleman)'.

But Dad was on the edge of the new family, however kind and loving that family was, and he felt the need to prove himself. He was the only one who went to the Ipswich Grammar School. This must have cost a farm labourer's family more than they could easily afford, and much was expected of him. I know he found it difficult to study in a home where study was a novelty and no provision was made for the work. He once told me that he did his homework on the kitchen table while his mother was ironing at the other end; and no doubt the other children were either crying or playing around him.

He was his mother's favourite child, as, unfortunately, boys tended to be at that time. He wanted to make his family proud of him.

"I left a good home, mother ... an excellent stepfather ... but I do my best in training ... and I know that by God's help I shall win through and make my dear ones proud of me."

Doubtless his apprenticeship had demanded the same high standards of him as he demanded of himself. He told me that he spent the first two years learning how to sandpaper properly. He had come to expect that everything had to be perfect for him, and that included his family as well as himself.

This striving for perfection meant that nothing short of it could be allowed, and reaching perfection takes time. Dad once started to make me a desk from the uncut wood to the finished article; it was never completed. He built chicken runs for my sons: never completed. This 'never completed' was the bane of my mother's life; the good intention was there and the skill to accomplish the end, but it had to be perfect if it bore his mark. Dad often found himself striving for the impossible.

The flip side of his temperament was that he had to deride the success of those who had achieved it in whatever field. As it happened, once I had learned to read – more of this in the chapter called 'School' – comprehension was considered by my teachers to be a strong point of mine. Comprehension was the ability to understand texts, sentence structures and elements of grammar. Books filled with comprehension exercises were part of our staple diet, and I enjoyed them.

Dad must have come to hear of this and ever after if I failed to grasp a new idea or appreciate his understanding of an old one the comment would be:

"That's comprehension. That's comprehension for you. That's comprehension in the real world."

There was no pleasing him. The secret of finding peace and contentment for oneself was to give up trying, but it took me a long time to learn this lesson.

He was a man of his time – many fathers were like him in those days – and he was a man of the war years. That generation of men had fought a vile and bloody conflict to secure their country's freedom and create a better world for their families. It is hardly surprising that they felt embittered on their return: the 'homes fit for heroes' never materialised and those who reaped most of the benefits were those who had stayed at home 'looking after number one', as Dad used to express it.

During rationing you could 'always get a decent steak at the Ritz' and 'High Court judges were not eating Spam ... they were getting pork and beef from their estates'. Immediately after the war, shortages and rationing was made more difficult as a result of the 1945 dock strike. For people like Dad, this severely tested his idea of working-class solidarity.

"The working classes are their own worst enemies," he would say.

By going on strike, the dockers made life hard for ordinary people. He believed in union power, supported the idea of the Welfare State and resented the fact that working men couldn't see that by sticking together and behaving responsibly they could change society for the better. By the same token he admired the toffs for looking after their own kind.

I gleaned his views over many years from exasperated comments, verbal explosions and random accusations against union leaders and politicians who let working people down. *Was it here I became a socialist with a small 's'? Yes it was here.*

My overriding picture of Dad during the Turin Street years is of him standing at his bench in the shed he built in that small back yard. He is wearing a white, carpenters' apron with large pockets more or less all round. A joiners' pencil – one of those soft-leaded, oval-shaped pencils – is behind his right ear and he is smoothing a piece of yellow-white timber, which he has secured in his wooden-fronted vice, with a block plane.

The shavings, each one a perfect curl, are dropping to the floor at my feet, and I am looking up at him and watching them fall.

Dad smoked heavily all his life – everyone did in those days – and Mum did at that time, although she gave it up many years later. Typically, she gave up smoking overnight – just like that! Stubborn, see! Once her mind was made up, there was no going back: no patches, no long consultations involving a doctor's time, no appointments with the nurse, no expensive products to help, no government-funded adverts and kits. Just willpower! That generation had willpower. *Is that where I learned to stand on my own two feet? Yes, it was there, thanks to my parents.*

Despite my parents smoking there was never that awful, acrid smell associated with smokers in the house, and I do not recall the presence of many ashtrays or yellow ceilings. Perhaps Mum kept the windows well open – fresh air cured most ailments in those days. Dad often said he couldn't afford not to smoke because naval cigarettes were so cheap: one shilling (5p) for twenty RN cigarettes in the white packet with the blue labelling. I was never tempted by my parents' habit – partly, I think, because I knew they would disapprove if I did start smoking and I would have to endure long lectures from my father about why I shouldn't be indulging. I was attracted by the pipe however, and always admired Dad when he had his briar clutched between his teeth. My grandfather gave me a small, used pipe of his and I sucked on that for years.

My parents smoked but they did not drink. I think few people did in the 1950s: there wasn't the money and there wasn't the availability. People would buy in port and sherry at Christmas and beer was available in pubs and from off-licences, but Dad frequented neither of these establishments. When at Westerfield, he would go to The Swan and have a drink with his father and friends, but drinking wasn't a habit of his in the 1950s.

Neither was gambling, unless the football pools come into that category. The law considered them to be 'a competition of skill, rather than chance' and so they infringed no legislation. Coming up on the 'Treble Chance' was the ambition of most men and Saturday evenings were always tense with excitement as Dad checked off his coupon, hoping for the eight draws needed to win a fortune on Littlewoods Football Pools. This was Dad when his sharp humour was at its best and we enjoyed the thrill with him.

My thirteenth birthday present was a bicycle, and it was Dad who taught me to ride. I believe we had moved to Gleneagles Drive by April 1957 because I can recall him taking me along the Westerfield Road, sweating and panting as he grasped the seat while I tried to attain my balance. He was very patient and I was a slow learner: my sense of balance has never been good and my spatial abilities are poor. Once I had mastered the art, however, I cycled everywhere possible and became both confident and adept. Punctures were common but never a problem: every boy could mend a puncture in the blink of an eye. The roads were fairly clear of cars in those days and the chances of an accident minimal, especially if I kept to country roads; the towns, anyway, bore few cars and the main danger on those roads were lorries, trucks and buses. The bike was a Raleigh with a Sturmey-Archer three speed gear; it was red and white with a well-sprung, tan-coloured saddle and a matching tool bag. It was a heavy bike, but very stable; it had a dynamo with a small wheel that I rested against the rear tyre when I wanted lights. I loved it; it brought freedom to go further afield whenever I wished. I have a vague memory that it cost £20. What Dad earned I do not know, but a farm labourer in those days was on about £6 a week and a teacher in 1966 was on £11 a week; by any estimate, then, the bike was worth about two or three weeks wages.

One of Dad's interests was breeding birds: first goldfinches and, later, budgerigars. He had no room for an aviary at Turin Street and so he built one in the backyard of his parents' home at Westerfield. It was, of course, a superb aviary: solidly built, wind and water proof, spacious and well designed. You could walk into the aviary without disturbing the birds and reach the nest boxes likewise.

I admired the goldfinches tremendously; there can be few more beautiful birds than this finch with its red face, conspicuous yellow bar on the black wings and the black, white-tipped tail. The red, white and black pattern of the head is particularly distinctive.

I have an extensive knowledge of British birds through very little effort on my part. I did possess the *I-Spy* book, but it was from my father and maternal grandfather, casually and on walks, that I picked up most of what I know in a very random manner, *and I am grateful for this lesson in how children learn through interest rather than cramming facts.*

Dad's ambition was to breed a perfect grey and a pure albino budgerigar. Albinos are sometimes produced as freaks; Dad's intention was to produce such a bird consistently. I understood at the time that there had never been a perfect grey strain of budgerigar; offspring tended to revert to the traditional blues and greens.

The Royal Navy both made and marred my father. It was a total way of life, and he never settled to the slap-dash ways of Civvy Street. If he had had his way, the home would have been run like a ship. (I know one ex-naval man who actually had 'Orders of the Day' pinned up on the wall of his house.) Mum would not hear of it.

"You can't bring the navy into the home, Wal," she would often say.

In his heart, I don't really believed he wanted to do so – Dad appreciated the comforts of his home – but he knew no other way of conducting his life and he brought naval attitudes to bear on his relationships. He tended to talk to people as if they were commissioned officers or ratings below him in rank and for whom he had responsibility. Aboard a Royal Naval ship, discipline is not lax but it is relaxed. I know this from the many times I have been with Dad to his various 'ships' (A shore base is still referred to as a 'ship', hence *HMS Ganges.)* There is both an abruptness and an ease with which naval people talk to each other, but we were too young as children to understand this fine distinction. When he spoke to us, as he would have addressed a fellow sailor we took him literally and not metaphorically; it was an order, not a query or an encouragement.

The attitude brought an expectation of obedience to discipline to bear upon the home: nothing was spelled out and no hand or voice was raised but we knew what was expected. This may work very well aboard ship or in any establishment where the ultimate authority figure is at a distance, but when it comes to family relationships and personal dealings with people on a one-to-one basis a gentler and more intimate approach is needed.

Did I learn from this? Yes, I always valued the central role of good discipline in my schools, but my handling of individual pupils was altogether softer.

We were nor a religious family; we never went to church and nor was religion discussed in the home. Again, there was an expectation that we believed in God. When I raised a question on one occasion, my father's response was immediate.

"You're Church of England until you're twenty-one."

Twenty-one was the age at which we were considered to be adults and could make free decisions on our own behalf. This was a widespread fact; even at teacher training college in 1966 we were expected to be in by 11 o'clock at night: no exceptions.

There was, of course, never any discussion in our home – religious, political or otherwise: the view of the man of the house was always right. Whether Dad actually believed that to be true, I doubt, but it was always enforced and stifled any possible discussion of any subject on which our views might differ from his. This may sound 'Victorian' but many of my friends experienced a similar attitude; it was an attitude that led to the rebelliousness of the 60s.

My mother, I think, was a quiet atheist; the idea of there being a god meant nothing to her. Dad was different. He went to church aboard ship because it was an expectation. His god was, I think, Blake's 'Ancient of Days', a truly fearful figure presiding over Earth, Heaven and Hell. But Dad wasn't frightened of Him! He had fought a war, 'done his bit for his country' as he wrote in his diary and although he respected authority he wasn't prepared to be bossed around by the church or the state. The war was the beginning of the end of forelock tugging: you obeyed those in authority over you but they were no longer considered to be your betters. Fate had found a new place for you both.

Neither one of my parents ever said that they loved us, but we knew that they did. *Nowadays, the word has been reduced to the meaningless: everybody is always saying 'lots of love' to everybody else, and so, in the end, the word will have no special meaning at all.* In the 50s, it was a declaration imbued with meaning: intimate, exclusive, personal rather than social, a commitment for life. Understandably, it was hard for such reserved people as my parents to make such a declaration, but they didn't have to do so: unspoken though it was the reality was there and they showed it in the only ways they could – through deeds and actions.

Studio photograph, circa 1945

Chapter 4
The Wardens of Bath Street

The Wardens lived at number three, which was at the top of the street. At the bottom was the River Orwell, where we took trips on a steamship called the River Lady and where Mum learned to swim when a girl. During the floods of 1953, as a child of nine, I stood and watched floodwaters surging up Bath Street and pausing just before they reached my grandparents' house. This was fortunate because, although the house was several high steps above pavement level, the kitchen, scullery and pantry were in the basement. Had the floodwaters reached number three, they would have poured down through a grid; and below stairs was cool and damp enough at the best of times.

I was fascinated by the basement. It was accessible from the hallway of the house and from an additional flight of steps that led from the backyard. We rarely, if ever, entered Nana Bathstreet's house through the front door; it was usually by walking along the passage that separated them from the Eagle Tavern. Always, but always, I wanted to descend to the basement rather than ascend an equally steep flight of steps to the back door. The basement was ill lit and there was a spookiness about the three rooms that I found attractive. They all led off a short corridor. Looking back and up I could see the light from the house above. The only light in the basement rooms seemed to come from the grid at street level. The floors were stone slabs. Large saucepans hung from hooks in the walls and from wooden rails. A clothes rack was raised by pulleys to the ceiling. The scullery seemed lined with cold slabs. Along one wall was a gas cooker.

Passing from here to the rest of the house up a flight of stairs we came to the hall. This emerged near the back door. The living room went off to the right, and this looked out over the garden. A grandfather clock stood against the wall. Tick, tick, tick, tick: the rhythm was steady. There was a clock in every room of the house, but this was the most impressive. My Grandad would take a large key and wind this one up. He also did something to the pendulum, but I was never sure quite what; chains were involved and a gentle rasping sound. He seemed to wind every clock in the house before he went to bed, opening the glass fronts and shutting them with a gentle click. There was something very relaxing about the rhythmic ticking of those clocks; it never sent me to sleep, but instilled a sense of peace and quiet.

There was a slight turn in the hall beyond the clock, and this part, which led to the front door, was curtained off. The room there we entered only with Nana and only to look. It was Nana's front room, as precious as Mum's but containing a married lifetime of paraphernalia. It was furnished with a three-piece suite, a china cabinet or two, low tables with round tops on which stood a plant in a china pot, high tables with round tops on which stood a plant in a brass pot, a flower-patterned carpet, velvet curtains across the bay curving to a fold, net curtains across the windows, and – yes – here an aspidistra flew. A canary sang from its cage. The mantelpiece was festooned with china ornaments, among them a white spaniel with a brown tail. I hate to say this, but I will: because of its position it always seemed more like a large lump of poo than a tail, and I came to dislike the spaniel. But there were bells to take my mind off the dog and little, painted and varnished cottages, hiding something behind their front doors. The mirror reflected this array of a lifetime's sentiments and I could see myself admiring them. Pride of place was bestowed on two matching china dogs, each with a black and gold collar and an orange nose. It was rumoured that these were worth a fortune, but like most rumours it wasn't worth the waste of breath needed in the telling.

Leading up from the main hall was another flight of stairs to the landing for the bedrooms. Mum told me that we had slept at Nana's on occasions (although I don't see why since we lived only five minutes' walk away in Turin Street) but I have no recollection of this part of the house. Sometimes, when chasing around with my cousins, I would run up these stairs, but only so far. Nana wasn't over the moon about children running round the house, anyway, and the dark halfway up was hiding place enough.

The living room was the one we knew best as children. It was here that the uncles, aunts and cousins gathered.

Before we take tea with my grandparents, let me introduce the Wardens. Mum, born Edna Florence in 1916, had two sisters, Lorna and Irene, and two brothers, Fred and Eric. My grandparents' names were George Frederick and Anna-Maria, whose maiden name was Last. My grandad was always called Dick by everyone outside the family and my grandmother was called Nell, and this was one of the puzzles of my childhood: no one knew the reason. To us children they were known as Grandad and Nana Bathstreet to distinguish them from our grandparents at Westerfield who were called, similarly, by where they lived. Between them, the three girls had nine children and Fred had five with his wife Jean. Eric was a bachelor.

At one time or another, many of us would be gathered in the living room in Bath Street for Sunday tea. This was a ritual of my childhood. The table on which the food was spread was pushed to one side creating a large space in front of the fireplace. In winter, a fire would burn here and in summer its place would be taken by an aspidistra. The surround was red tiles with a wooden mantelpiece. A low, protective shield of brass and black-painted metal ran round the actual front of the fireplace; there was no guard as such. Grandad always sat in a low armchair to the right of the fireplace with one of us children on his knee. Nana presided on an upright chair to the left at one side of the table. Those children not in the place of honour sat on the hearth rug in front of the fire, while the adults sat where they could: on chairs round the table or on other chairs dotted about the room. We children, then, were the central focus of attention.

Tea was eaten from plates on our laps; there was a formality about the proceedings despite the casualness of the eating arrangements. For me, the centrepieces were the trifle and the salad. The salad was constructed in a similar manner to my mother's: layers of lettuce, tomatoes, cucumber, spring onions and radishes, sometimes topped with hardboiled eggs. Salad servers plunged into this work of art would produce a delicious and varied spread on your plate. The spread was laced liberally with salad cream.

There were always additional salad items for those who wanted them, and one memory distinct in my mind is of Uncle Fred shaking the moisture from a salad leaf onto the floor. He always smiled when he did this, and I wondered at the time whether it was something he had been forbidden to do as a child or whether he was teasing us children by spreading the drops of water over our heads. Uncle Fred had a quiet smile that could have indicated simple happiness or could have hidden some reflection he was not able to share at the time. The gentleness in his eyes drew us children to him. He was a slight man, similar in build to his father, and his children adored him. Years later, when I was working on the Christmas post, I bumped into him on the Maidenhall Estate, and asked about his family.

"Jean left me," he said, "some years ago. My daughter, Julie, stayed with me and has looked after me." It was typical of the times that my mother had never mentioned to me that her brother and his wife had parted. Uncle Fred was as quiet and unassuming as always, referred to me as "boy" and praised his daughter to the skies. I thought it typical of her that she opted to look after her father.

But in the early 50s we were gathered together and Jean was part of the family. Teatime at the Wardens was a quiet affair: sometimes so quiet you could hear the clock in the hall ticking. If anyone had anything to say, they said it and everyone else listened without interruption: there was no vying for precedence, no attempt to top someone's story with another. It was always easy to get a word in and the family showed an interest in what each person had to say. *Was this where I learned the art of listening to a line of argument, to follow a conversation through and build a complete picture of the event in my mind? I don't know, but having a family who were attentive must have been a great start.*

Nana and Grandad Bathstreet with Lorna, Edna, Irene, Fred and Eric

There were sandwiches: cucumber, egg and cress and Spam sliced thinly are the ones I remember. There were Suffolk scones, congress tarts and coconut pyramids. And there was the trifle – ooh, the trifle! My mother must have learned how to make a trifle from Nana Bathstreet. The same care, the same attention to detail was apparent in both: too much cream, too much custard and you end up with a sloppy mess, stint on the fruit and it no longer deserves the name of trifle. This never happened when I was a child. The base always seemed to be a jam-filled Swiss roll, which was moistened but not made soggy with the fruit juice from the tins of fruit. Tinned fruit was a luxury, but it seemed to be available; it was often apricots, and these were spread over the roll. Next came a layer of jelly followed by a layer of custard; the jelly kept the fruit and roll from becoming soggy. This arrangement seemed to be repeated until the top of the trifle bowl was reached, when a layer of cream was added. This was sometimes dotted with hundreds and thousands or sliced, fresh cherries in season. I also seem to remember – but I could be wrong: it's a long time ago – that a layer of crushed ginger nut biscuits played a part somewhere in the wonderful confection.

We all loved trifle, and no wonder. It was the crowning glory of Nana's Sunday teas. Uncle Eric was no exception. We followed the example of the adults and always called him Uncle Tubby. He took no offence: being fat in the 50s carried no particular social stigma and fat people felt no particular anguish. Looking back I can see that Uncle Tubby was fat, but I never noticed it at the time. All fat men were called Tubby, and being our uncle the title suited him. Like Dad and Uncle Fred he had been in the Royal Navy during the war and he served in the submarine service. I was introduced to him at five months old through *Good Morning, the Daily Paper of the Submarine Branch*. The article runs:

> 'Here's a photograph taken ... at your home ... Your mother's canary livened up proceedings with a burst of song ... Let's start off with a message from your mother. You are always in her thoughts and she hopes very soon to see you walk in and have you sitting round the table with the family, like the good old days ... Your dad is ever so well and still working. Sisters Edna and Irene are

cheerful as ever ... and young Terence is too. True he had no smile for the photographic occasion, and probably was disappointed not to see something funny pop out of the box. Whatever his thoughts your young nephew kept them to himself. By the way, isn't this the first time you've seen him?'

Whether that cheered him up, Uncle Tubby never said, but when he smiled he chuckled. He lived at home until he moved to Station Street, near the family home, when the house was eventually sold. I never did find out what he did for a living, but that was typical of the times: grown-ups never told us anything.

Nana would always pour the tea, and it would be from a china teapot into a china cup. Balancing the cup on your saucer was an art a child of the fifties had to learn. The tea was made from loose tea leaves, which would be spooned into the pot; once brewed, the tea was poured through a strainer into the cup and onto the milk, which had already been poured from the milk jug. It was not considered good form to pour the tea in before the milk. The tea was always a nice red-brown colour, not muddy as some teas now look, and it had a sharp, clean taste. Until children had learned to like tea, they would be offered fruit juice drinks: Robinson's Lemon Barley Water was the most common, and we all loved Ribena, but this was on the expensive side. Most people took sugar in their tea, and the Wardens were no exception. My dad always had two spoons of sugar. To keep the tea warm in the pot, Nana used a tea cosy, probably one she had knitted from scraps of wool. My mother had several.

Nana Bathstreet was partially deaf, and this affliction runs in our part of the family: my mother was stone deaf by the time she died and I am going deaf. We learned to speak slowly and clearly when talking to Nana and it was important to face her when we spoke so that she could watch our lips. We also learned to raise our voices, but not to shout. *Was this where I learned to speak loudly and clearly? I think so.*

Nana was a very self-contained person: so much so that she verged on being reserved. There was nothing standoffish about her manner, but she stood and sat upright and smiled rather than laughed. Her eyes looked straight at you. Her smile was of the sort called 'demure', and it gave the impression that she was weighing you up: I was never quite sure what Nana was thinking. She also dressed in a very precise manner: her brooches, for example, were always 'just so', as the saying goes. One piece of clothing I always associate with her is a fur coat, which had padded shoulders; this gave her a rather military look. Whenever she was out, Nana wore a hat and it was always set at a jaunty angle with great care and held in place by a hatpin. The one I associate most with her was made of felt; it was round with quite a large brim and the hatband was decorated with flowers.

Nana and Grandad Bathstreet on a stroll along the Ipswich docks, 1935

The Warden girls were all loud: they spoke loudly and laughed loudly. Aunt Lorna, the eldest sister, was the loudest of all. You couldn't but like Aunt Lorna. She was a jolly person who would have made a good landlady; I believe she did work behind a bar at one time. If you did anything wrong she would say: "Don't you worry, boy. You aren't the first, and you won't be the last."

When I was in the Cubs and Scouts, she always gave me a job during Bob-a-Job Week. It was never difficult, but I felt I had earned my money. She lived on Heath Road, near to where we moved in 1957, and was married to Fred Heath, who worked in a garage. Uncle Fred collected motorbikes. I imagine he used the parts to repair and re-construct others. Whatever the motive, when the bike was no longer of any use he buried it in the garden. Like many people in those days, he did the best he could with what he could find. He also kept chickens to help feed his large family. There were five Heath children: in order of age they were Derek, Doreen, Peter, Mary and Colin. Doreen was nearest to me in age.

When he left school at fifteen, Derek got a job at Ransomes and Rapiers, a firm close to where we lived that made farm machinery. (It was used as the location for the 1960 film, *The Angry Silence*, which was about a man sent to Coventry by his workmates because he refused to join an unofficial strike.) Mum and Aunt Lorna must have got together to ensure he had a decent dinner (which we ate at lunchtime), and so Derek came to us. I must have been about eleven at the time and so Derek seemed a man. He would enter by the back door, take off his work boots and join us for the meal. One week, he didn't hand Mum the money she and Aunt Lorna must have agreed as payment for the lunch, and still hadn't by the Tuesday or Wednesday. I don't suppose the small amount of money involved was important to Mum, and it was the 'principle of the thing': the principle that it would do Derek no good to get something for nothing. Whatever the reason,

Mum was annoyed. I heard her teeth click and I heard her voice upbraid Derek. He rose from the table, walked into the kitchen, calmly laced on his boots (resting his feet on the back door as he did so!), smiled at me who stood open-mouthed watching him, gave me a wink and left. He never came for lunch again.

I learnt nothing at that moment – I was too startled – but I admired the audacity. Thinking about the incident many years later, I realised that Derek would have rather eaten in the works canteen or taken sandwiches and enjoyed them with his mates on the Orwell quay than come to his auntie's for lunch. He was fifteen, he was becoming a man and he had broken free. When I spoke to him about the occasion at his mother's funeral in 2012, he was embarrassed and said:

"I expect I apologised for my behaviour afterwards." *But need he have done so? Haven't the young the right to break free?*

Shadows would lengthen over Sunday tea in winter, but it was always cosy by the coal fire. Grandad would light his pipe, after knocking the old ash out on the side of the chimney breast. Sometimes, we would play board games on the floor; at others, we listened to the grown-ups talking, but they always brought us into the conversation somehow. Grandad would also read stories to us, and the grown-ups listened to them. If we went over nursery rhymes for the younger children, everyone would join in. There was lots of laughter and clapping of hands.

Being so close to my grandparents' home when we lived in Turin Street meant that I saw a great deal of my grandfather. He would take me for walks on a Sunday morning, and he was a quiet man. *When you are with someone who chatters incessantly there is no time and space to absorb the atmosphere of all that surrounds you: chatterers are a constant distraction.* With Grandad I absorbed a sense of place: the river, the docks, the parks, the Strand. I can picture them as clearly today as I did when I was a child. He talked, of course, of birds and flowers, of where we were; without realising it, I was filling my mind, and later my imagination, with those pictures that would form such a vital part of my memory.

The day came, however, when – like Derek – I had to break loose; I must have been fifteen by then, and we had been living at Gleneagles Drive for about two years. Grandad had caught the bus into town and out again so that we might continue our walks. This time they would have been across Rushmere Heath and the surrounding lanes and woods.

"I don't want to go out with Grandad anymore," I said to my mother, one morning. I don't recall her answer, but she must have spoken to my grandfather and we never walked again. I have no idea what reasons she gave. I realised that I would have hurt the old man's feelings and, although I realise now that he and Mum should have anticipated my need, I always regarded what I had done as a selfish act because he had been so kind to me. *It's just one of those regrets that, after a lifetime, you take with you to the grave.*

Grandad and Nana Bathstreet were a devoted couple. Even if divorce had been a possibility for their class of people in those days, it would never have crossed their minds. They walked out together, and in the few photographs I have they always appeared to be rather dapper and content in each other's company. As I have said, Nana took considerable care about her appearance and Grandad resembled H.G. Wells. People didn't drink much in those days, but they must have frequented the Eagle Tavern, which was next door, because I have a photograph of them sitting, leaning, against the bar. Grandad, with a pint of beer behind him, is wearing a flat cap and smoking his pipe; Nana has that Mona Lisa smile on her face and is wearing her fur coat. In another photograph, she is pictured with a host of other women, posed in front of a coach before an outing from the pub.

Pubs in those days were dingy places, full of smoke and with rarely a woman in sight. For some reason, I was allowed in once. It was a place of scrubbed deal tables, dark beamed ceilings and mainly men sitting round with their pints of beer, smoking and playing cards or dominoes. I cannot recall why I was there. Perhaps it was a festive evening: often a musician – a singer, piano player or fiddler – would entertain on a Saturday night. I was transfixed by an Irish tenor. He was a sharp-faced man with sleeked-back hair and a tight mouth, which opened down to the left as he sang. In his hand he held a pint of something with froth on the sides of the glass. I couldn't take my eyes off him and he seemed to be staring at me: perhaps a child's fascination flattered and captivated him. He sang such numbers as, *I'll Take You Home Again Kathleen, The Rose of Tralee* and *Galway Bay. The beauty of traditional Irish songs, despite their sentimentality, haunts me to this day. What's wrong with sentimentality, and why is it always seen as false?*

Although we lived fairly close to each other, getting such a large family together for an outing must have been a challenge: people moved around using buses and trains because cars existed only for the wealthy. Everything needed for the day had to be packed and carried. Apart from buckets and spades, towels and costumes, this would also have meant preparing and packing the day's food and drink. Ice creams would have been available but there were few cafes and they would, anyway, have been too expensive. I have a photograph of nine of us Warden grandchildren on Felixstowe beach, a seaside resort about ten miles from Ipswich. Getting there would have involved either two buses or a bus and a train and a long walk from Felixstowe station to the beach.

With us are Nana and Grandad, Aunty Jean and Uncle Fred, Mum and Aunty Lorna: missing are Dad, Uncle Fred (Heath) and Aunty Irene and family. Dad was almost certainly stationed away from home and Uncle Fred (Heath) was probably at work. There was no sick pay in those days: if you didn't work you didn't earn and the family didn't eat. Doreen and I are standing at the back; Doreen is leaning on Nana's deckchair and I am shivering under a towel. The girl in front of Grandad is Mary and the girl in front of Mum, who is sitting next to Nana, is my sister, Linda. Aunty Lorna, an unnatural blonde, has Peter and Colin to her right. In front of her is one of Uncle Fred and Aunty Jean's boys. Jean is nursing her youngest child and her oldest boy, Francis, is sitting in front of her. Uncle Fred took the photograph, but appears in the companion shot.

This would have been a long and exhausting day for the grownups, but we looked forward to our days out. Holidays, either at home or abroad, were a rarity for working class families but people were determined to enjoy themselves. The grown-ups had lived through the hardships and atrocities of the war and were experiencing the austerity of the post-war years. Our country was bankrupt and in debt up to the hilt to the United States. Our parents and grandparents did not dare think about what the future might hold for them or for us; they wanted to live for the day and were grateful for what little life had to offer.

Being part of such a large family did have its drawbacks, of course, especially for the younger children. Since times were hard and clothes rationed until 1949, mothers were of the generation who had learned to make-do-and-mend: nothing was wasted and our mothers welcomed hand-me-downs, which we had to endure. I recall my school uniform and a Sunday best suit, which was similar to a grownups but with short trousers.

As we grew out of these, they were recycled and would be used with a cousin's left-off jumpers and shirts when we went out to play. Mothers were adept at darning anything made of wool, such as socks and pullovers, and patching everything else. Mum, having been trained as an upholsteress, was Queen of the Patches: on jumpers, jackets and trousers her patches were almost works of art. Something being full of holes was never a reason to throw it away: it would 'come in somewhere'. We never had newspaper in our shoes like some children, but ours were always bought 'with plenty of room to grow into' and were only replaced when our toes were nipped tight.

One hand-me-down to which I had a strong objection was a jumper that must have been knitted for my cousin, Doreen, who was slightly older than me. It was a beautiful jumper in the style called Fair Isle, but it was obviously a girl's because it had puffed shoulders. Mum assured me that it was a good fit and that I looked smart, but the shoulders were too much to bear. Rather than go out wearing it, I somehow acquired a pair of scissors and cut a one-inch snip in the bottom. The wool began to unravel and I pointed this out to Mum. She, of course, must have realised that the cut was a cut and not a tear. Her teeth clicked a few times and I braced myself for the slap round the head, but she said nothing and the jumper vanished from my life.

No one in the neighbourhood looked down on us for the way we were dressed because everyone was subject to the same privations. In fact, anyone having a change of clothes for every occasion would have looked the odd one out.

Grown-ups, too, wore their clothes until their clothes wore out. They bought few new clothes for themselves and looked after the ones they possessed. Every item was carefully removed, brushed clean and placed on a hanger or folded neatly. What they did have new was often homemade on the family sewing machine. Every mother owned a sewing machine and would scour the glossy magazines for ideas, producing outfits for themselves as well as their children.

The Wardens – woman, man or child – were always well turned-out, irrespective of whether the clothes were darned, patched or homemade. In the case of my sister and me, our mother saw to our being 'presentable in public'. My father, too, was particular about the way he looked: if he had been gardening and needed to go to the shops, he always changed into more suitable clothes, however immaculate he had been dressed for gardening. In his case, it was a combination of personal pride and his naval training; in my mothers, pride had its place alongside the family example set by Nana and Grandad Bathstreet.

Nana and Grandad Bathstreet

Chapter 5
The Daveys of Westerfield

My father's father was killed in the First World War, and no one ever mentioned this happening: the only information I had about him as a child was a large photograph on the living room wall at Westerfield. He is standing in a photographer's studio in front of one of those backdrops; he has a baton under his right arm and has placed his left hand on what I take to be an artificial wall. He is extremely smart (his shoes gleam with polish), and has what appear to be exceptionally long fingers, although this is not a feature passed down through the family. The eyes are my fathers, whose birth certificate states that William Ernest Cant was a farm labourer.

My grandmother, Nana Westerfield (born Florence Frost), later married Henry Davey, who was always called Harry; in fact, I never realised his actual name was Henry until I saw his gravestone in Westerfield churchyard. To all intents and purposes, Harry was my grandfather, and I always thought of him as such, just as my dad always looked upon him as his father.

Harry, or Grandad Westerfield as we called him, was also a farm labourer, and their house was a tied 'cottage'. It was a semi-detached house called Elm Villa; the 'Elm' was acceptable since one grew at the top of the garden but 'Villa' was certainly a misnomer. It had a front room and a living room with a kitchen no larger than a galley, downstairs; upstairs, reached from a large hallway, there were three bedrooms, the smaller of which was converted into a bathroom once the children had grown up and left home. Like us, when the children were young the family would have strip-washed in the kitchen or with bowls and jugs of water in the bedrooms.

In the yard there was an outhouse that contained a large, stone copper, which was fired by coal, where Nana did the family washing and the washing she once took in from people in the village. Behind this was the toilet; there was no indoor toilet when I was a child. A large shed-cum-workshop stood on the other side of the yard, behind which was a barley field separated from the yard by a hedge and a ditch.

We would catch Cecil Osborne's coach from St Margaret's Plain to Westerfield, and my parent's instructions were always the same: "Top of the hill past the Swan." It wasn't, of course, Cecil Osborne's coach but I always thought of it as such and he always looked after it as though it was his own. He dropped us opposite the garden gate and we walked down the path to the house. In summer, my great-grandfather, 'Gaga' Frost, would sit outside the front door awaiting our arrival and always ready for a game of dominoes.

The garden was very long and stretched from the front of the house to the main road. There were apple trees, a vegetable garden and a pigsty. We plucked and ate gooseberries just as they ripened in summer: sweet they were, turning from green to a translucent yellow. There were raspberries, too, as I remember, and there was always a great deal of fuss about cutting down the raspberry canes to within a certain height above the ground.

Windfalls were common as the apples ripened and treated with unusual contempt from people who wasted nothing.

"You don't want them old windfalls, Edna," my grandmother would say to my mother, "Harry will pick you some fresh fruit."

Harry did. He placed a ladder against the trunk of the tree and reached into its branches to pluck the ripe fruit, while I stood below, holding a wicker basket as he passed the apples down. It was here I learned to climb trees when I was old enough. There was one at the top of the garden on which someone, years before, had placed a horseshoe that was now embedded in the trunk.

The windfalls were not wasted, of course: they were enjoyed by the pigs, as were the peelings and outer leaves and skins of everything Grandad grew and we ate. He mixed these scraps with some brown meal he measured from a sack and mixed the lot with hot water (I think it must have been hot, although I never saw him heat it). I would lean over the pigsty and watch him pour the slop into the trough. The pigs would then shove in their snouts and slurp away until it was consumed. They loved apples just as they were, picked from the ground and tossed into the air for them to catch or placed into their mouths.

There was an old carter in Westerfield at that time. He would pass by the garden gate and we could hear the clip-clop of his horse's hooves on the road. My father always told us to look out for any droppings the horse might leave as these were good for the garden. The carter had a livid red face and a shock of thick, white hair. I asked my father why this was so and he replied that the man had been struck by lightning. It didn't really matter whether or not this was true: it was the stuff of storytelling.

My father's boyhood home at Westerfield was a fascinating place for me as a child. I loved going there. *Later, the countryside and Westerfield were to play their part in some of my novels: Rebecca Unwood's love of flowers, Corvin's walk, Brultzner's flight and Sarah's ecstasy in* The Vampire's Homecoming, *the farming scenes in* The First Rendlesham Incident, *the railway station in* The Age of Wisdom *and the hippy scenes in* Swinging in the Sixties. More than this, our visits to Westerfield gave me a feel for the countryside.

The living room was the centre of the social life of the house; here a fire was lit in winter and it was the only warmth in the house. A huge table dominated the room: a table so large that it would comfortably seat two at each end and five along each side. The result was to push every other item of furniture back against the wall. My nana had an armchair by one side of the chimney breast and on the other side was a store cupboard. To reach this it was necessary to climb onto an enormous sofa that was squashed against the end wall and on which whoever was eating at that end had to sit. Along the side wall opposite the fireplace, situated between the sofa arm and the window, was a massive radio set. I think the speakers must have been situated beneath the dial. The casing was wooden and it stood as high as the table. Twiddling the dialling knob to tune in the stations was the job of my Uncle Ken.

Everyone had their place at the table and my Uncle Ken always sat at the far end. On his left, on the fireplace side, sat my grandad. Nana reached the table from her armchair. I always sat at the far end from Uncle Ken and my mother and father sat with their backs to the window with Linda next to them.

Ken was the kind of uncle of which every child dreams. He never stopped chattering during meals and the chatter was directed at making us laugh. It was very child-like humour in which he indulged. If our cousins were with us, his excitement was quadrupled. His chatter was a mixture of quips, family gossip and questions about what we were doing. His chatter included reminiscences about the family history or anecdotes about people in the village. He was much attuned to any particular gathering and selected those stories or comments that would rouse a mixture of laughter and hackles. He also sprinkled his monologues with words that children automatically find funny: sausages, drawers (an old fashioned word for knickers), belly and bottom are a few I remember. He would also embarrass us by asking if we had 'a girlfriend (or boyfriend in my sister's case) yet'; the word 'yet' held the expectation that we would soon, should have or were slow on the uptake. Ken, himself, never married.

His humour was undoubtedly of the music hall kind and involved a good spattering of double entendre that was above the heads of us children, but this kind of crude humour went down well with everyone: the Daveys were a family that would enjoy the *Carry On* films of the 60s.

My grandad would sit quietly, an elusive smile on his face, while my nana would be chuckling away; my mother also seemed amused, while my father looked as though he was putting up with his half-brother's humour. At some point, as Uncle Ken's excitement grew, Nana would say: "Drarp it Ken do!" while often chuckling almost hysterically.

When this had gone on for a while, my grandad would raise his knife hand a fraction and say: "Gurrn yer!" and everyone would laugh.

If Uncle Ken continued, Grandad would eventually reach for the large leather belt around his waist and looked as though he was going to remove it, at which stage Uncle Ken would raise his hand as though in defence. Grandad never did remove the belt and all the while this pantomime was in progress the laughter expanded around the table.

Uncle Ken often included his mother in his humour: sometimes as an arbiter of opinion, sometimes as the butt, as men do when fond of their mother. When she was included, he always referred to her as 'Florrie', as did my father. It always shocked me that a son would refer to his mother by her pet name rather than as 'mum', but it was the case. I could never imagine my father doing anything but frown had I referred to my mother as "Ed".

Nana Westerfield was born Florence Frost and her family came from Swan Lane in Westerfield; the lane still runs down by the pub. She was a fat woman, sat around a lot, and moved with difficulty; this was how I saw her when a child. When we went over for tea, she made no attempt to prepare anything, but would wait for Grandad to come in from work. After a while, she would say: "That celery needs doing, Harry."

In his own time, my grandfather would rise and begin preparation of the celery, and then my mother would go into the small kitchen and help. Nana Westerfield never moved from her armchair at the corner of the table. She was always dressed with a smock covering her clothes; at the time I never wondered why. I remember thinking that all fat people were inherently lazy and quite happy for others to rush around on their behalf.

The cloth would be spread and the food placed upon it. I have no clear recollection of what this was but salad was there and plates of some meat – probably corned beef – and a plate of buttered bread. There was always plenty of bread, and my grandmother's skills as a hostess came into their own at this moment. She would remain seated, tuck the loaf under the pit of her arm and proceed to slice the bread with the requisite knife. I always admired the skill involved in this art; if you wonder why, try to cut slim, even slices of bread in this manner. The butter was in a dish and spread easily with a single stroke of a knife across each slice; the butter was a creamy yellow against the white of the bread.

Grandad and Nana Westerfield had two other children besides my dad and Ken. Both were women: one was my Aunty Barbara and the other my Aunty Ivy. Barbara had married Horace Fairbrother and they had two children, Barry and Jennifer. We saw a great deal of them at Westerfield. When we were all there the table was crowded and some of us had to sit with our backs squeezed against the fireguard. In winter, with the coal and log fire roaring up the chimney, this position soon grew quite uncomfortable, but any complaints were always treated with a laugh.

"It's all right, boy, it'll do you good," Nana would say, although I never fathomed quite how this might be.

"It's better than being cold," was another truism of hers that was not particularly helpful, but we all had a good laugh and it was always said in the best of spirits.

The table came into its own during the evening when the grown-ups would play cards. The main game was Newmarket. One pack of cards is used and one player per game is dealt a dummy hand so that a number of cards remain out of play for

Grandad and Nana Westerfield

that round; this becomes the dead hand. Should the player dealt the dummy hand not look at it, then it can be bought by another player in which case his or her original hand becomes the dead hand. Three cards are chosen (from another pack) to be used as 'horses'; these are usually a Queen, a King and a Jack. At the start of each game, players place a bet on the horse of their choice and put some money in the kitty: we played with a penny and a halfpenny. Play commences from the player with the lowest black. Players must follow suit until no more cards can be laid. Then the player who played the last card leads with their lowest red. The purpose is to play any horses you may hold but this is often made impossible because of the dead hand. The first player to get rid of all their cards wins the game. Another is then played. Money not won on the horses remains and so builds up through the evening.

It was a most exciting game, not because of any great skill involved but because of the chatter that ensued with each round of cards. It was always aggravating to almost, but not quite, be able to play a horse; it was also exciting to watch the money pile up on the horses. Sometimes the kitty was not won because no one had a low red or black to lead, and so the money piled up here as well. No one ever won or lost a great deal but when we children were old enough to play it was exciting to gain a whole pile of pennies.

I say 'when we were old enough to play' because during the years we were considered too young we were ignored, and expected to play under the table. Quite what we were expected to play was not clear; the main thing was that we were out of the way of the adults. Every now and then, Nana would say: "Are you together all right under there?"

We always said we were, and when the grown-ups topped up their drinks we were offered lemonade or squash. It was an adult-centred evening at Westerfield.

Elm Villa attracted many visitors, and one of these was Beattie Barber. The grown-ups never explained who Beattie was or from where she came. William Cant's mother was a Frances Barber and a man we called Uncle Herbert was also a Barber. He and Beattie were related in some way, but it remains a mystery as to how. I always understood that Beattie was one of my father's aunts. She enjoyed a game of cards but was reputed to cheat. On several occasions I heard my grandmother say, with a chuckle: "You're cheating, Beattie."

This could have been my grandmother's perception of how Beattie was playing her hand: perhaps Nana Westerfield wasn't able to play her horse. I don't know, but the allegation always caused amusement and Beattie never denied the allegation. Usually Uncle Ken diffused any spite with, "My God, Beattie!" and that was that, as they say.

Beattie was a spinster and tight. My dad and I went round to her house to do a job – replace a tap washer or something – and asked for some water to wash our greasy and dirty hands. She heated the water in a kettle and gave us half-an-inch in the bottom of a bowl.

Aunt Beattie expected to be kissed when we left her house, and I always hated this moment because she had a permanent pimple on her chin where my lips would land. After a while, I developed the simple expedient of being last in line to pass her as she stood in the doorway. I would then nip behind a chair and manage to slide out behind her. I never felt guilty about this strategy. Eventually, her pimple disappeared. The story went that she had rubbed it with red meat, but this might just have been a story.

Another visitor, not this time a family member but a friend, was Kenny Clemence. When Kenny was due, it was roll out the red carpet time. Uncle Ken was always anxious that things should be just right for Kenny, and the best tea service was apparent on the table. He struck me as odd in that I had never met anyone quite like him. Kenny had left the village and 'made good in London'. What he did, I have no idea; it was simply an achievement to have left Westerfield and been successful in the outside world, and this is what Uncle Ken both admired and envied. In his heart, Uncle Ken knew he would never leave the village. Kenny Clemence was, therefore, a role model. He struck me as odd because of the way he walked in little steps and the way he sat upright at the table instead of leaning forward on his elbows. Kenny Clemence could converse with anybody: the farm labourer or the museum curator. He spoke not so much with a posh voice as with an affected one, as though the tone had been carefully cultivated. He dressed immaculately in a snugly fitted suit or blazer and a lilac shirt: at least, that is how I remember him. When he used his hands to gesticulate, the wrist was always limp. He came from a village family and was always welcome at Elm Villa when he returned to see his mother who still lived in Westerfield. Whenever Nana spoke his name it was always with a certain reserve. Her tone was not scathing but cautionary and I could not understand why at the time. He took little interest in us children but was always polite and most solicitous to my grandmother. There could not have been a greater contrast in style and dress than that between this man and my family.

Grandad Westerfield always seemed to be in the same clothes, unless he was dressed for an occasion, when like all men of his generation he was really smart: pin-striped light brown three-piece suit, watch chain, brown brogues polished to a high shine, starched collar and tie and the nattiest fedora imaginable. Otherwise, it was corduroy trousers either tied at the knee with string or secured with spats and held up with braces, working man's boots, check shirt, battered fedora, old waistcoat, a wide belt that was there but seemed to serve no purpose and the item I remember most – a red neckerchief tied in a loose knot. This he removed when he entered the house; out in the fields it no doubt caught the sweat of an honest man's labour. He worked all his life as a farm labourer, raised a family of four children and never obliged his wife to go out to work; he died with one shilling and sixpence to his name. I know this because my father told me in a tone that showed his grievances against the unfairness of the world. *Were my political allegiances being further forged here? I think so.*

Although we called him grandad, we – my sister and cousins and I – thought of him as Harry. He was quiet, but not in the thoughtful way of George Frederick Warden: Harry Davey's quietness was purposeful, focussed on the job in hand. He didn't appear to ruminate like my other grandad but was all consumed with the moment. *I didn't know it then, being a small child in the presence of an adult, but it was here that I learned to focus totally on the task in hand; this ability has served me in great stead all my life – as a headteacher in particular but also in completing all I have ever set myself to do on time, and in coping with an innate shyness socially.*

Harry's shed-cum-workshop was a ramshackle place, as I have said, and we children were told to steer clear of it: there were tools in there on which we might cut ourselves. Besides, the concrete floor was badly cracked and holed in places and this was where the rats came through: 'rats as big as puppies'. The rat story was true. When I was tall enough to reach the Suffolk latch I did venture into Grandad's shed with its cast iron roof and I saw the rat holes and the rattraps.

It was Grandad who showed me how they worked. Some rattraps are circular in shape and made of wire. In the centre is a hole through which the rats enter after the bait, and because the wire ends stick downwards the rats cannot escape. Such a trap would catch several rats. Another type is a smaller version of the old mantraps once used against poachers; the jaws are pulled back and clicked in place, the bait is placed on a weight-sensitive plate and the rat's weight releases the jaws, often cutting the rat in half. It was brutal, but kinder than filling their bellies with Warfarin, which brings about days of agony before the creature's final death.

It was in this shed that Grandad taught me how to pluck a pheasant. It amazed me to see just how many feathers there are on a single bird; they flew everywhere, covering floor and bench tops and wafting up my nose and in my hair. Afterwards, my appreciation of the meal itself was enhanced tenfold. Roast dinners were commonplace at Westerfield: the meat, rabbit or game bird, was shot and all the vegetables came from Grandad's garden. It beat rationing and cost the price of a cartridge. I am a vegetarian now, but as a boy I tucked into roast meat with the best of them.

"You be careful, son," my dad would say, "You don't want to bite on any pellets."

I also learned to shoot in the field behind my grandad's shed. There was no fence between his backyard and the field and the hedge was down at this point. He had a 410 shotgun, the stock of which had been made by my father. It was a beautiful piece of woodcraft, polished and fitting snugly into the shoulder. My dad showed me how to aim, allowing for the kick of the gun when fired, and I practised on tin cans. It was exciting to see them leap into the air from the tree stump when the shot hit them. Eventually we went into the field itself and searched the hedgerows. The rabbits kept clear of us, but eventually we came across a bird – I think it was a hedge sparrow – chirruping on a branch. The aim was easy and with the natural spread of the pellets it would have been impossible to miss. I might not have killed the bird, but it would certainly have been maimed. I remember feeling, quite distinctly, that I had no right to fire the gun and end this bird's life. It would have been pointless, since the little creature would have been too small to eat. I aimed, raised the barrel above the hedge and pulled the trigger. The hedge sparrow flew away, a song on its beak.

"Never mind, Son," said my dad, who was with us at the time, "Better luck next time."

I looked into his face, ashamed at my own ineptitude, but I saw no recrimination there, more a sense of relief.

Bird nesting was another matter. My cousin, Barry, and I collected birds' eggs by the dozen. The rules were clear: only one from each nest, as long as there were several there, and never disturb a hen bird on the nest. We scoured the hedgerows behind Elm Villa, and Dad made me a little box, which he lined with cotton wool, as a secure place to keep the eggs. I forget which nests we plundered. Only three come to mind: pheasants, blackbirds and robins. I remember the pheasant's egg because it was large, the blackbird's because they were easy to collect and I loved the brown speckles on the green-blue background and the robin's because of the beautiful pale blue colour. I kept them for years together with a book called *Eggs and Nests of British Birds*.

Country life is different. Even in those days, the town dweller saw only the carcases hanging up in the butchers' shops: pigs and, sometimes, rabbits. What we never saw was the killing: the pheasant dropping from the sky, the rabbit twitching in the air, the pig's throat being cut. In the countryside, people become hardened to these horrors. Harvest was a dangerous time for rabbits, in particular.

When my mother was about to deliver my sister in 1951, I was sent away to live with a friend of my parents. This lady I called Aunty Betty, and it was she who persuaded me that I liked tomatoes simply by encouraging me to try one. Aunty Betty was married to Cyril Garnham, and they had two sons about my age, David and Richard. They lived in East Bergholt, and behind their house was a harvest field. I think the crop was wheat, and the combine harvester was working its way round the field from the outside in. We children had a great time. We were encouraged to help with the harvest by moving the bales of straw to the burgeoning haystack. A ladder was placed against the stack and we mounted this and assembled the bales as the stack got higher and higher. Of course, at the end of the day the farm hands removed the ladder, pretending to leave us there, but it did not seem to matter: straw is soft and welcoming.

For the rabbits, however, their day was drawing to a different close. As the combine closed in on the centre of the field they had nowhere to run except out and across the open stubble towards the hedge, and this is what they did. We were handed sticks and rakes and branches – anything that hands could be laid upon – and told to man the hedge. As the rabbits raced up and down, we stood at the gaps ready to club them to death. I saw many but could not bring myself to strike at one. The country folk did, however, and by the end of the day the poles they carried home were lined with corpses.

I never experienced anything similar at Westerfield. The nearest I got to death was the report of my grandad's shotgun and the sight of a rabbit twitching in the air for the last time.

Rabbit in the stew pot is the sweetest of meats. Among the vegetables sprinkle a few sultanas and they enhance the dish no end. We ate this with mashed potatoes and greens from my grandad's garden and it cost the family next to nothing.

It is generally acknowledged that country folk fared better than townsfolk during rationing, and this was certainly true of Westerfield in the early fifties. My family had friends in and around the village, and one of these was the Coles of Pip's Farm. They were friends not relatives but we still called them Uncle Percy and Aunty Eva. They had a son, Ian. They were generally considered to 'live on the fat of the land' as my mother put it. Certainly, at their house Ribena was poured as readily as Robinson's Lemon Barley Water at ours.

"Would you like a glass of Ribena?" asked Aunty Eva whenever we arrived, and we certainly did.

We drank it sitting in their huge kitchen with the thirteen cats under the large table, warmed by the Aga stove in winter and summer alike. Aunty Eva always seemed to be standing at the kitchen table dishing out food to us or to the animals. Who else in the 1950s could have afforded to keep thirteen cats? One of them was named after me – Terry – but he was aloof and I found it easier to befriend Ian's cat, Mickey, a large black and white creature who was, according to the tales, a 'great mouser'.

Pip's Farm was named after one of their dogs, and it was a wonderful place to be as a child: the freedom was limitless. We explored fields, barns, farm machinery and abandoned tennis courts. There were pigsties and stables in which to play and create games. There was a stagnant pond where we tried in vain to catch tadpoles, and there was the house itself. The front door opened onto a wide hallway that led to a cloakroom. A cloakroom! We lived in a house that didn't have an indoor toilet and Ian's family had a cloakroom that included a downstairs toilet in addition to the one upstairs!

But we never felt daunted: Aunty Eva and Uncle Percy were too unconsciously generous to engender any such sense. Uncle

Percy had a car – a Ford Consul – and he was quite willing to drive anybody anywhere. At night he would return us to Elm Villa or even home. I watched him from the back seat with a child's eyes full of wonder as he dipped his lights or changed gear with a lever on the steering wheel. Cars were unheard of among people of our class. The only people who owned cars were doctors and posh people; but Uncle Percy wasn't posh. He was an ordinary, working farmer.

The Coles dressed well. I remember my mother's annoyance when Aunty Eva said that Ian had six of everything: six pairs of socks, six pairs of pants, six vests, six shirts and – possibly – six pairs of trousers. This meant that he never had to wear the same clothes two days running no matter how many were in the wash or how many he got dirty. For most mothers in the 1950s it was usually two of everything: one on and one in the wash. Given that wash 'day' was as I have described when writing about my mother's week, the implications of this do not need much imagining. It was a matter of pride to have three of everything – the third being one spare.

I felt ashamed for the first time in my life at Pip's Farm. I had been to one of Ian's birthday parties, and Aunty Eva was nothing if not generous. When we came to leave, she had prepared a goodie bag of gifts for each of us to take home, and these lay waiting on a table in the comfortable, spacious front room. The bags were not all the same and I think I must have been attracted by the ones that contained a particular gift. I forget what the gift was: it may have been a rubber ball. Anyway, as Aunty Eva handed me my gift, I must have 'put on my parts', as parents used to say. I clearly did not want that bag and must have said so. I can remember Aunty Eva's voice saying: "Well, do you want it or not?"

She spoke with some asperity and well she might to such an ungrateful child. I forget whether I took the bag: my shame at my ingratitude overwhelmed me.

I did not learn shame from any religious precepts, but knew instinctively that I was in the wrong. *From where did this early display of conscience come? Was it from somewhere in my upbringing or is it part of the human psyche? If so, then it divides us as a species because I have met people with no conscience at all.*

It is generally assumed that after the war attitudes began to change quite rapidly. Young servicemen returning home were no longer prepared to doff their caps or tug their forelocks to those who had once been seen – and seen themselves – as their betters.

> 'The rich man in his castle
> The poor man at his gate
> He made them high and lowly
> And ordered their estate.'

This verse was dropped from *All Things Bright and Beautiful* long before I began to sing it as a child; in a version I have of *Hymns Ancient and Modern*, published in 1950, it does not appear. The attitudes, however, remained, although this may have been more apparent in the countryside than the town.

Living in the village at that time there was a lady who everyone referred to as Miss Jean Waters. My father once explained to me that she was 'a lady'. This was not a reference to her moral status but to her class. Miss Jean Waters was seen as belonging to a class of people quite distinct from our own. I recall vividly an occasion when my father must have been asked to go round to her house, which was called Sarony, and undertake a job she needed doing. My father was no doffer of caps and believed fiercely in the rights of the workingman, as I have explained, but he was flummoxed on that day. It was clearly an honour to be asked to undertake work for Miss Jean Waters. He was always particular about his appearance when in public, but especially so when he visited Sarony. My mother checked that he looked 'all right', he checked the state of his tool bag, my grandmother burst with pride as he made his way up the path to the gate of Elm Villa and he was bursting with pride on his return. He talked about it for a long time that day and I was informed that Miss Jean Waters wanted to meet his family. He was, remember, a boy from the village who had made good: he was a craftsman, had signed up before the war started and was still serving his country in the Royal Navy. Miss Jean Waters had obviously known him as a boy.

I don't recall the details of her house – perhaps I was overwhelmed or perhaps she met us on her driveway – but I can recall standing by the white fence that broadened out as it met the road, and I can recall the lady. She had one of those cut glass accents that make you feel uncomfortable when young; she was petite, genteel and courteous. She was also genuinely pleased to meet us and clearly proud of my father.

Was it here I learned to judge people on their merits rather than on their class? Yes, it was here. Years later, when I defended toffs at college to my socialist friends I was chaffed. I was given to understand that allowances couldn't be made in the class struggle – and I can see the point – but it wasn't what I felt and still isn't.

This attitude to class was never more apparent than in a person's dealings with the church. All clergymen in those days were from the upper middle classes, at least. *As recently as the 1990s, it was difficult for a working class man to gain a foothold in the priesthood. I know this from one who succeeded.* However friendly they were, clergy seemed a bit aloof from their parishioners simply because of the way they spoke.

Even those people who never attended services felt obliged to respect the church and the clergy, children were still automatically baptised and most people were married in church; a registry office wedding didn't seem to be a proper wedding. There was an incipient pressure still exerted to attend church, and everyone had what was called their Sunday best. When I was thirteen, my father said: "It's time you got yourself confirmed."

This was despite the fact that he had never taken me to church and without explaining how I might achieve such an end.

Such was the situation in Westerfield as I experienced it at that time through observation rather than intellect. I heard the rector's voice, I saw the deference accorded him when he visited Elm Villa, I watched him listening with patience to whatever my grandmother had to say, I noticed the awkwardness with which my family entered the church, I heard the irreligious asides and I noticed the concern that we should be seen to be respectable. *None of this was formed into an opinion, of course; it was simply stored for later use.*

Nana Westerfield must at one time have been a regular churchgoer because the rector visited regularly and seemed familiar with her and her ways. I got the impression that she had once organised such things as jumble sales and whist drives. He was a friendly man and always accepted a cup of tea when he called.

In such areas the church retained its traditional role as a focal point in the community: it was a meeting place, a social outlet, an arbiter of disputes, it welcomed us into the world and eased us out. Priests such as the one I saw talking to my grandmother knew their parishioners and touched them deeply at critical moments in this lives.

When my father applied to join the Royal Navy, the rector gave him a reference.

'*Dear Sir,*

I have known Walter Ernest Cant for about eight years. He has been living in the parish all his life. I believe him to be a very suitable candidate for the Royal Navy. I have much pleasure in recommending him to the Naval Authorities. I believe he will do well.

Yours faithfully,
C Boorman
Rector of Westerfield'

Whether the rector availed himself of Elm Villa's toilet facilities I doubt. There were not designed for guests of any standing, although they were considered to suit the family admirably. Our outside toilet at Turin Street was left in the shade by the one at Westerfield: we, at least, had a cistern and a chain to pull. The only toilet at Elm Villa had neither. A wooden lid with a large hole shaped in it closed over a large, cast iron bucket. There was no electricity linked to the toilet. This was the case at Turin Street but the lack of light seemed infinitely worse at Elm Villa. The door at home did close and lock, but here there were gaps beneath and around it to let in the draughts as I sat with my trousers round my ankles. The place was also damp, and blackened spider's webs hung everywhere. Under the seat around the bucket there was a huge amount of space where any creature might lurk. As the day wore on the smell became unbearable despite the natural air holes in the door. The smaller you were the worse the problem: actually hauling oneself onto the wooden lid and hanging one's posterior over the large hole was a major undertaking and there was always the fear that you would fall into the bucket and the shit. I can recall leaning forward in some trepidation to reach the toilet paper (always Izal and always hard on the wipe) and then easing myself back with one hand desperately gripping the lid and the other gripping the paper. I won't go into the difficulties of using Izal: let's just say it was hard, non-absorbent, slippery and brittle!

What did I learn here? Was it to conquer one's fear of the unknowable? There could be any number of spiders beneath the seat just waiting for a pair of buttocks, but one could never know for sure and so it was best to just get on with the job as quickly as possible because the job had to be done.

Uncle Ken was the one who, in the morning every morning, saw to the bucket. Night soiling it was called and was supposed to produce excellent rhubarb. I never knew where he buried everyone's excrement but it was somewhere in the garden.

It was as I grew older that I began to see another side of Uncle Ken. If ever we stayed overnight, the boys, Barry and I, sometimes together and sometimes alone, would share his bed.

It was quite common in those days, when guests were staying, for up to four to sleep in a double bed, sometimes head to toe. In this way, I became familiar with his room and his books. The *Teach Yourself* series, with its black and yellow covers, dominated the shelves, the windowsill and the top of the chest of drawers beside the jug and water bowl, which were ready to receive the hot water for the morning wash. You could, in theory, teach yourself anything from these books: self-defence, biochemistry, astronomy, ethics, psychical research, sex: its meaning and purpose, political thought, to name a very few. Uncle Ken felt ignorant and was eager to learn. I found it bewildering that an adult felt ignorant. It was only later I realized he had probably left school at fourteen with only an elementary education: reading, writing and arithmetic.

Enough to make him easily governable but insufficient to allow him to think, debate and form ideas of any profundity for himself; his education was not designed to create an individual ready and able to challenge the existing order. But that idea came much later – not from me but my friends at college.

At that time, I merely felt sorry for the man. He asked endless questions to which I was only glimpsing the answers myself. My own learning and, therefore, my thinking was in its infancy. I gave him what answers I could but always left him feeling I had been less than adequate. *Was this where the idea I might learn and teach was forged? I don't know. My world was probably opening up at my secondary school but I had far to travel.*

My grandfather's death was the first in which I was involved, however slightly. We had moved to Gleneagles Drive by then and I had my bike. My parents had been called away to Westerfield one morning. My sister tells me that Uncle Ken arrived with the news and that Mum wept: this was unusual for her, a woman later noted for her stoicism. By late afternoon they had not returned. I must have been worried because I cycled over to find them. When I arrived, Nana was sitting in her usual place but not in the armchair: she sat upright at the table and was smartly dressed: the smock had been discarded. Around the room sat relatives I had met occasionally but did not really know – Olive and Bert, who shared a house but were not married, and people from the village. The rector, I was told, had just left. They all seemed pleased and surprised to see me and I was told that my grandad had just died.

"Do you want to see him, boy?" I was asked.

"No thank you," I answered, and they all laughed.

There was an atmosphere of deep respect in the manner of these people and in their dress: all were dressed in black and all wore an expression of quiet acceptance on their faces. Even when they laughed it was in a quiet and dignified manner. Watching them and trying to understand my nana's question, I realized that my grandad was laid out in the front room: the room where Uncle Ken played the piano. I could see him in my mind's eye: the hawk-like nose, the thinning hair, the quiet smile, the work-worn hands and the strong line of his jaw.

I didn't feel it right to see him. I don't think it was fear: I cannot recall being nervous. I think it was the surprise and a lack of understanding. Thinking back, I consider my 'decision', such as it was, to be wrong but I cannot return now.

I remember him most vividly when he took his storm lantern, which creaked as it swayed in his hand, and led us to the top of the garden on a dark, winter's night. We would stand just inside the gate by the tree with its embedded horseshoe and he would stand on the road. As Cecil Osborne's coach was glimpsed approaching from the direction of Witnesham, Grandad Westerfield would wave his lantern to flag it down. It would take us into Ipswich and drop us on St Margaret's Plain from where we would walk home.

Nana Westerfield with her father, 'Gaga' Frost, and Beattie Barber's sister-in-law, Lily, and Barry, outside Grandad's shed where he taught me to pluck pheasants

Chapter 6
School

I loved school. To me it was a place where I met and made friends. It was an introduction to and an extension of the streets on which I played. Learning had little or nothing to do with it until I was thirteen in 1957, and by then it was too late.

Luther Road Infant School

My first class was Miss Pullin's, who lived opposite us on Turin Street, and the main attraction was her spaniel, which wandered the classroom, up and down the rows of desks, waiting for one of us to offer her a biscuit. My mother wondered why I showed no interest in taking a mid-morning snack after we left Miss Pullin's class, but she knew nothing of the spaniel's existence.

Luther Road Infant and Primary was, in fact, two schools with two headteachers. Miss Northfield was head of the infant school, which was on the ground floor, and Miss Hack was head of the junior school on the first floor. It was a modern building of its day, built with spacious corridors so that it could be used as a hospital in the event of another war. The classrooms adjoined the corridors and each one was shut off by a heavy, metal, sliding door.

We sat in separate wooden desks each with a lid that was raised to reveal its contents. In the afternoon, once we had returned from lunch, we laid our heads on our arms on the desk and had a little sleep. Only the poor kids stayed for a school dinner; the rest of us left at noon, walked home and returned for the afternoon session at two o'clock. Afternoon school finished at about four o'clock.

I think I was probably well-behaved on the whole, but there was one occasion when this could not have been the case.

"Do you want to stay in after school?" asked the teacher.

I took this as a threat that I was to remain in school all night. Much as I enjoyed being there this thought held no appeal, and when afternoon playtime arrived I made my escape. I recall quite vividly hiding behind the toilet wall. The toilets were at the end of the playground overlooking the long driveway that led to the wrought iron gates. The wall of the toilet was curved and I pressed my back against it so as not to be seen. Once the bell had been rung and the other children had filed in I ran hell for leather up the driveway. It was probably a mile to our house: up the drive, down Luther Road and Station Street, along Wherstead Road, up Kenyon Street and turn right into Turin Street. Home!

I have no memory of what happened when I arrived. I must have explained why I ran home, but whether my mother was angry, upset or relieved I have no idea. I do remember Miss Pullin coming over to our house in the evening and talking to my mother. Years later, my mother recalled Miss Pullin's words:

"He ran like the wind," she said, "We had no chance of catching him." It seemed to end harmoniously. I have no memory of any rancour towards me or towards the school. It was just one of those things that, fortunately, ended happily for all concerned.

I have always disliked uniforms and I believe this may have started at school. We were obliged to wear white shirts, grey worsted short trousers (designed to be of use as playing out clothes when we had grown out of them), a school tie with matching snake belt, a blazer and a matching cap. I did quite like the tie and belt; it was the cap to which I objected most strongly and the restrictions of a blazer in summer. I recall my mother arriving at school with a clothes prop to recover my cap from beyond the railway line fence. I can recall throwing it over, but cannot imagine I would have admitted this to my mother.

I have no other memories at all of my time at infant school, which must have spanned the years 1949 to 1951. Whether this is because one day was much like another or because I was off school for much of the time with childhood ailments, I have no idea. One thing I do remember is that I arrived in junior school unable to read, despite having enjoyed my early years being filled with fairy stories and nursery rhymes. Someone had failed to teach me that essential skill that opens so many doors and roads, but this might have been due as much to my absence as the teachers' ineptitude.

A brief sojourn at East Bergholt village school
Before moving to junior school at Luther Road Primary, I spent some time at the village school in East Bergholt. This was during the time my sister was born in June 1951. How long I spent there I do not know, but I suspect it was a few weeks at the most, and of that school I have sharp memories.

The desks were heavier and appeared to be bolted to the floor. I recall wood and iron. The teacher – an old lady in a cardigan – sat at her own desk, which was similar to ours but higher, and spent her time knitting. I was fascinated by this activity and can recall thinking that it could not be right, although I had no idea why at the time. I can see, even now, the busy movement of her knitting needles and the occasional glance she bestowed on the children. The classroom was dominated by the sound of those needles, which echoed in the silence.

A young girl paraded between the rows of desks, helping us when we needed it. Who she was, I have no idea: an older pupil, a student teacher, a helpful parent – who knows, but it was she who did the work.

The playground buzzed – boys roared and girls screamed – and there was a sharp, distinct contrast between this and the classroom. I was staying with my Aunty Betty (not a relation but a friend of my parents) whose older son, David, was about my age. I have no memory of him in the playground, but I recall being surrounded by older girls who seemed to want to protect me. There was a great deal of fussing and guiding, and I recall the pleasure I felt when they leaned over me asking questions. It never occurred to me to postulate the idea that girls are nosier than boys – although I later found this to be true – but I did enjoy their attentions.

This was a country school with country children and country evenings. The days in the classroom with the high windows through which you could see nothing were interspersed with time in the wheatfield, the hedgerows and the cricket pitch. White and yellow and green were the colours of those few weeks. I was running free and the warm smells of summer were in my nose. *Was this where I developed a love of village cricket and the countryside? Yes, it was here.*

Luther Road Junior School

Mrs Lewis was the Baptist minister's wife, the mother of David and the teacher who taught me to read at the age of seven. If I had to choose just one teacher from the many who I came to respect it would have to be Mrs Lewis.

I remember sitting alone with her in the classroom, during what must have been her lunch hour or playtime break, with a book in front of me. The book was one of the old, much-maligned *Janet and John* series. Thank you, Janet, and thank you, John: you were there when I needed you! Mrs Lewis is listening to me read. She has black hair, greying at the temples, which is brushed severely back and held tightly by a ribbon or stretch of elastic. She has a nose slightly turned up at the end with wide nostrils. She is wearing a purple cardigan. Since I went home for lunch this must have either been just after all the other children had left or on my early return, and probably by arrangement with my mother.

It doesn't really matter. What does matter is that Mrs Lewis took that bit of extra trouble to ensure that I could read, however late in the day at the age of seven. Once I had learned, I never stopped reading until I became a father and ran out of time at the end of each day. Enid Blyton's *Secret Seven* were my first solo ventures, and at last I could read the narrative under the rhyming couplets in my *Rupert Bear* stories. Comics became comprehensible: I journeyed into space with *Dan Dare* and rode the range with *Jeff Arnold*. By the time I was eleven I had read *David Copperfield*.

Later, I was to write my first adventure story about a character called Jeff Dare. I have no idea who he was or what he did but his story was the only piece of school work in which my father showed an interest and it was written because we had a new teacher for a while. Again, whether Mr Bingham was a student teacher on a supply teacher I do not know, but he inspired me to write. I think the Jeff Dare story received one of my few gold stars for good work. Together with Mrs Lewis, as far as I was concerned Mr Bingham stood out among the teachers at Luther Road Primary.

I took a liking to few others. Mr Taylor was obviously ex-army: I could tell that at the tender age of somewhere between seven and eleven. We would be marched down to the playing field and he would pick the usual two boys to be captains of the opposing football teams. Once the twenty-two had been selected, the rest of us would be tossed a ball and sent to play on the 'bottom pitch'. There was no attempt at coaching skills: we never learned how to kick a ball, how to pass, defend or attack, how to play our positions on the pitch, what they meant and what we were intended to do.

Those of us on the bottom pitch learned what few skills we acquired through the aggressive play of Alex Kennedy. Once Alex had the ball, it was a foolish player who attempted to take it from him. He would power down the pitch towards the opposing goal, the ball at his feet, muttering: "Fuck off, fuck off."

SCHOOL

(It was the only time I heard that word throughout my life until I became a headteacher myself and had to ban two mothers from the school premises for using it: one was a governor and the other a mother known for her foulness of mouth.) Needless to say, we kept out of Alex's way and learned to pass rapidly if approached by him on the pitch.

These 'matches' – if I can grace them with the name – were always played in flimsy shorts and football shirt. No matter how cold the weather or how wet or how windy, we bunched together in a straggled group until chosen or rejected and then ran around trying to keep warm. Even the goalkeeper was not allowed a track suit. This sort of bull was a result of the war years, of course: it smacked of the army. The idea was that we must not be allowed to grow up soft. We had to be toughened up, hardened off. It never actually occurred to anyone that we might enjoy the sports more if we were warm; but even if it had, the facilities were not available. There were no showers in those days, even in a modern building like Luther Road, and so we clambered back into our uniforms, muddy and wet and raw with cold during the winter months.

The only sporting activities I enjoyed were the ones associated with summer, Danish rounders and athletics, although as far as the latter is concerned running and jumping would be a more accurate term. I also enjoyed PE, particularly what was called Swedish drill. We stood in straight lines, forming the vertices of a grid, sufficiently far apart so we did not knock each other, facing the teacher who made a series of movements that we copied. It was not unlike Zumba dancing today in that a large number of people aped the movements of the one facing them. There was a great deal of arm and leg swinging so that our bodies resembled a mass of Xs at times and a great deal of stretching up and to the sides; but there was no pressure on the individual to shine or, alternatively, make a fool of themselves. The synchronised movements involved similar skills to those involved in courtly and country dancing.

Was it here that I began to develop a love of the mathematical nature of such dancing and a dislike of team games? Yes, it was here.

The only other teacher I can recall who made any impression on me was Miss Mauldon. She had a large, round facing imbued with a purplish colour and I swear she wore a hairnet (although this could have been my imagination). Whenever something needed to be marked or checked we lined up at her high desk at the front of the class. Why we couldn't have remained seated while she moved round the classroom I am not sure; perhaps it was connected with the British tradition of queuing. I always put off joining the queue until I could not decently do so any longer. Once you reached Miss Mauldon, her technique for improving your understanding was not complicated. Any failure on a pupil's part to arrive at the correct answer to an arithmetic sum was remedied by her picking the pupil up by the shirt and pullover and shaking them backwards and forwards. Whether or not this was intended to agitate the grey matter sufficiently for it to gain the necessary enlightenment I am not sure. What I am sure of is that it was quite terrifying to be suspended on tiptoes in this manner while her purple face exploded into yours.

This teaching technique apart, Luther Road Primary was free of any corporal chastisement; we were not regularly slapped, caned or slippered, despite the belief that this was commonplace in schools of the 50s. In fact, I cannot ever recall it happening. Discipline was implicit in the tradition of the school. Lessons were very quiet; children were not expected to talk. Much learning was by rote: times tables come readily to mind as being taught by this technique, but poetry, spelling ('i' before 'e' except after 'c') and the rules of grammar were instilled in the same manner.

I did not mind any of these attitudes to learning. It was always easy to stay quiet and still if you were unsure, and the rhythmic nature of chanting had a pleasant, corporate feel. To this day, I can recall speedily the multiplication of any two

SCHOOL

Class photograph, Luther Road Junior School. I am second
from left on the back row, John Hunt is sixth and Robert Harrison
far right; Jacqueline Kitchen is in front of me and Janet Ostler
stands to her left; Janet Squire is seated on the third row,
far right; Micky Warren and Roland Collins are sitting
cross-legged to the right of the board, 1955

numbers up to twelve times twelve and Wordsworth's *Daffodils* is a party piece.

An overwhelming desire shared by one and all was to be a monitor. Teachers loved monitors and forty pairs of hands thrusting into the air crying "Miss, Miss, Miss!" would have delighted them. One key monitor's job in the junior school was that of milk monitor, although others, such as pencil monitor (which enabled you to use the giant sharpener attached to the teacher's desk), offered their own attractions. The milk monitors' job was to cart the heavy, metal crates each containing up to thirty, one-third pint bottles of milk into the classroom. In winter, this also meant placing the crate near the one radiator in the room so that the milk would thaw out. I loved milk, and still do, and it was no hardship to me to suck the lumps of ice from the bottle if the milk remained partly frozen. The monitors were allowed to drink any leftover milk.

One unattractive monitor's job was to be the teacher's watchdog if he or she had to leave the room for any reason. This role was called the class monitor, and often undertaken by girls. *I have never worked out why this was so. Were girls more likely to "tell Miss" if any of us stepped out of line?*

Our real life at school was in the playground, and it was here that we learned about friendship. My friends of the playground were not necessarily my friends of the street (more of this in chapter 7). In the playground we tended to play with our own classmates, girls with girls and boys with boys.

I had a close friend for some while whose name was Micky Warren. We were both on the small side and I think that this must have been the initial attraction because, one day, a new boy, whose name was Roland Collins, joined the school and he was smaller than either Micky or me. Micky and Roland became instant friends and I was left in the cold. I can recall standing very lonely by the toilet wall of the junior playground and being approached by a girl whose name was Janet Squires (called Squirty Squires because she, too, was small), who commiserated with me. There's a sensitivity in women (not all, but many) about this kind of situation – the loss of friendship – and Squirty alone in that vast and noisy domain was there to say a few kind words. I think I was in love with Squirty for a while: I remember her and her friend, Janet Ward, with affection. A few school trips later and I found myself sitting near them on the coach; *but then women are good at that sort of thing too.*

I wasn't friendless for long, however. Other boys came over and soon I was in the thick of it. I think we raced around a lot early on in the junior school, desperate to emulate our comic heroes, and I can remember wishing away lesson time so that we could get on with the game. Roles were allocated on a smash and grab basis. In some groups I was Dan Dare but in others content to be his sidekick, Digby – but not as fat as Digby. It was a brave boy who offered to play the Mekon, but there were those who would and the offer brought with it immense credibility.

SCHOOL

We seemed to float in and out of friendships quite easily, and these depended on the nature of the game in hand. A current serial, such as *Rocket Man*, at Saturday morning pictures, or a Saturday afternoon film, such as *The Black Shield of Falworth* (1954), were capable of restructuring these groups rapidly. Girls were never involved in these adventures at school, and nor were some of the boys who always preferred to play football at one end of the playground.

By and large I do not recall much violence at school: there was the occasional stand-off between two boys but that is all. There was one incident, however, that has remained in my mind for the past sixty years or so. I was standing by the toilet wall talking to a new boy, Robert Harrison, when we suddenly became aware of a commotion. It appeared to be centred round one boy, always a bit of an outsider, who I will call Brian. A skirmish seemed to be about to take place when Brian ran off along the school side of the playground. He was immediately pursued by the group who had surrounded him. As the chase progressed, other children joined in: how many I do not know, but it seemed to be most of the playground. By the time Brian had reached the far end nearly every child seemed to be after him. He turned at the top and raced down the side of the playground that adjoined the field, as others were drawn into the pursuit. Finally, Brian took refuge by the toilet wall and the crowd surrounded him; there was no escape. He cowered there for seconds as the mob drew back. Into the space between them and the wall stepped a boy who I will call Cal. What occurred next happened so quickly that we were all taken by surprise. Cal walked up to Brian and felled him with one blow to the jaw. Brian was in tears, as well he might have been, and the look on Cal's face was as vicious an expression as I've ever seen on the face of any lout. Neither Robert nor I had taken part in this but I felt ashamed that I had not intervened in time; I never discussed it with Robert, but caught the look on his face.

It was definitely here that I learned to hate mobs and crowds. A vast group of people behaving as one are not driven by any clear thought or consideration for anyone else, but by a desire to behave collectively and appear at one with their friends. As long as an individual's behaviour coincides with what the group is doing, the individual is accepted by the crowd; if the individual stands against the crowds view, then the person will be ignored, at the best, or abused, at the worst. The incident also taught me that if most people 'think' that something is right it is almost certain to be wrong. Nothing I have seen or experienced in my life has changed the view I formed, however unconsciously, on that day.

By the time I entered junior school at the age of seven, I was making my own way backwards and forwards; it may have been earlier. On Station Street there was a baker's shop where a hot roll cost a penny. The smell was so enticing that many of us must have stopped to buy one, which we ate without adornment of any kind. I can still smell that shop now and feel the warmth of it as I entered, the bell ringing, on a winter's day.

Coming down the same street, one day, I was slapped across the face by one of the older girls. I didn't know her and have no idea why she took any objection to me. We must all have been on the way home when she came up to me, slapped my face and said: "You spoilt, little brat!"

Looking back, it must simply have been that she had started her periods early, such was her vehemence at a perfect stranger, but I knew nothing of periods at the age of seven: it was to be another thirteen years before I did.

I remember yards and yards of paper chains decorating the classrooms at Christmas and taking home next year's calendar that the teacher had made so that it might be perfect. A rectangle of cardboard was covered with a cutting of wallpaper, a pleasing picture stuck on the front, a piece of sugar paper covered the joins on the back and a little calendar was placed below the picture. *Was it here I learned that children must be allowed to make mistakes?* Probably not: my father would not have welcomed anything that was less than perfect. But I could see through the falseness of it all when my mother admired 'my' handiwork.

Christmas also meant the school play: as a cook throwing a bowl of rice pudding in the king's face, as the substitute king when the leading boy was taken ill, and then of being asked if I minded him having the cloak my mother had made for the part so that he could play it instead of me on his return. Did I mind? I imagine I did, and my mother even more so.

Did I mind Mrs Parry, who was responsible for the singing, telling some of us NOT to sing but mouth the words after she had placed her ear to our mouths and decided the sound we made was less than acceptable? Yes, I expect we minded both at the hypocrisy and the lack of coaching as to how we might sound better. But we said nothing – not at the age of 10 or 11. *We saved our minding for years later when we arrived back in school as young teachers and met the Mrs Parrys of the future.*

Robert Harrison came into my life at about the same time as another friend, John Hunt. I knew Robert was an intellectual long before I had ever heard the word or understood what it meant. It was not that he was simply intelligent, but that he could think outside the constraints of his own interests, concerns and current issues. Many intelligent people are quite without that ability. *Intelligence is common enough; an intellect far rarer.* I think at that time I must have been grasping at ideas that eluded me, but they were clear to Robert. He was also interested in gadgets. While the rest of us were hoping we might one day own a gramophone, he was already considering the greater possibilities of tape recorders. Needless to say, he went onto grammar school and our roads forked.

John was of a practical turn of mind. In his garden there was a shed that his father encouraged him to use as he wished. Together the three of us turned this shed into a submarine, a spaceship and ... I forget: it's a long time ago. In our creations we spent many a happy weekend, but it was John who was the leader: he saw bunks, control panels, steering devices,

My first *Rupert Annual*, 1948

periscopes and all in a piece of wood or the turn of a screw. I think I may have added the adventure and Robert foresaw, and overcame, the problems ahead.

Girls played their part but were not central to our lives; at that age we could well do without them. There was Squirty

Squires and Janet Ward and Brenda Cook who were fun enough on a school trip and looked attractive with the ribbons in their hair, but their interests and ours were elsewhere. There were girls we admired but who were outside our reach. Jacqueline Sharp, the blonde beauty of the class, was clearly within the range of Robert Broom, the most handsome boy in the class, but outside the scope of whatever desires might come our way. I fancied Jacqueline Kitchen: that wide mouth, those deep eyes and that lovely mop of wavy hair. But I didn't know what to do about my fancy and she always appeared to be looking the other way.

One girl stood out from the rest and I'll call her Harriet. At eleven, Harriet already had breasts. She was clearly years ahead of anyone else and Harriet was a very nice girl. I didn't fancy her in the way I fancied Jackie; my feelings for Harriet were ones of admiration. She stood out from the rest not just because of her physical development but because she had a posh voice: Harriet was decidedly in a class removed from the rest of us. She tried to make friends but the other girls tended to steer clear of her and the boys never understood her or were simply afraid. *If only, if only at the age of eleven we had a bit more understanding of others, how different our lives might evolve.* She sought me out and I never knew why; probably it was just someone to whom she could talk.

Our ways were, anyway, to follow very different roads. The 11+ exam saw to that quite decisively: the 11+ and the segregation of boys and girls into separate schools.

The one person not amazed by my failure to pass the 11+ was me. I had no idea what it was, what it portended or why we should be bothered by it. In November, we all sat in the main hall of the school, desks as wide apart as possible, while a teacher sat at a table on the high stage at the front. Silence reigned, but then it always did in school. It turned out later that we had taken the intelligence test. I must have passed this because in February those of us who had been successful went into the hall again and did some attainment tests. I imagine that these were English and arithmetic. I must have failed these – although how someone who had just read *David Copperfield* could fail to pass an English test must raise questions – because the following term my parents received notification that I would not be attending Ipswich Grammar School for Boys. I will never forget the look of astonishment on my father's face, but I was equally astonished that he thought I would have passed. After all, I could never remember gaining more than 14th place out of 40 on the class end-of-year lists: in those days, children were ranked (according to what criteria I am unsure, but it was probably English and arithmetic tests) from 1 to 40, which must have been pretty discouraging for those at or near the bottom of the list.

Years later, I did point out that if someone was intelligent enough to benefit from a grammar school education the fact that their attainment was poor must be the fault of the school, mustn't it? Of course, in those days schools were never deemed to have failed their pupils: but they did. Even had they not, however, the 11+ system would have done so.

It was another eight or nine years, after I gained a place at the County of Stafford Training College for Teachers, that I found out exactly how the 11+ selection system worked. A tutor explained that in counties like Suffolk there were 12 grammar school places out of every 100: so if, say, 25 pupils in any one year could benefit from such an education it was hard luck on 13 of them. In places like Monmouthshire, there were 40 grammar school places out of every 100; so if, say, 25 pupils in any one year could benefit from such an education it was going to be a hard road for 15 of them. I don't want to dwell on this gross, built-in unfairness and foolishness, but it is important to understand the benefits later made possible by the comprehensive system of schooling.

Those of us who ended up in secondary modern schools found them poorly equipped and unable to offer us any qualifications at the end of our time. We were denied foreign languages and all three of the sciences – physics, chemistry and biology – taught at that time: the money went to the grammar school pupils.

In addition to this iniquitous division on the basis of poor attainment at 11 years of age, there was another: boys and girls were also segregated. I can understand the distractions inherent in a co-educational system, but the advantages of educating boys and girls together far outweigh them. *When I see youngsters, today, walking to and from school together and when I witness the natural way in which they mingle, my heart leaps with joy.* In the 1950s a boy and girl walking in simple friendship would have raised eyebrows from the grown-ups and jeers or laughter from friends. Asking a girl out was an ordeal because you were approaching a virtual stranger, and not someone with whom you shared your schooldays. Girls were objects of wonder, put on a pedestal when their feet would have been better planted on the ground; being educated apart, we never came to understand or appreciate their uniqueness. Those of us who had sisters of roughly the same age were better informed, but not by much.

My mother's immediate concern was that I would end up at Tower Ramparts Secondary Modern School for Boys where, reputedly, newcomers were hung on the railings by the louts who had reached their final year. I doubt whether this was true but it might have been. Certainly, schoolteachers intervened less in those days: not one made any move to investigate the pursuit and crushing of Brian, for example. From her point of view, it was fortunate that I knew John Hunt. His parents were aware of a school in the town centre called St Margaret's Church of England School for Boys. We were not in the catchment area and we never went to church, but my mother must have applied and John and I were duly interviewed. I recall standing by the piano with Mr Baldry, the headmaster, and being asked to read from the Bible.

"In the beginning was the Word, and the Word was with God, and the Word was God. The same was in the

beginning with God. All things were made by him; and without him was not anything made that was made. In him was life; and the life was the light of men. And the light shineth in the darkness; and the darkness comprehended it not."

St Margaret's Church of England Boys School

I clearly found no problem with that reading, although John presumably did because I was offered a place and John must have gone elsewhere, and so, in the September of 1955, I went to St Margaret's. I do not remember that day but fancy I went alone. We would have done in those days. Cossetting was not in fashion; children needed to learn to stand on their own two feet.

I probably caught the bus from the stop near Uncle Tom's Cabin, a local pub, which was at the bottom of Vaughan Street, a stone's throw from our front door. Later, I was to walk across town to school: Stoke Bridge, past or through the docks, along Silent Street where stood the second-hand bookshop, through the Eastern Counties bus station, along the little road that led to the cinema in the Buttermarket, up Tower Street past the Ipswich Theatre, along Soane Street that ran between the posh teashop and Christchurch Park, over St Margaret's Plain and so to the school in Bolton Lane.

And all while reading a book! I never paused, I never looked up: I simply read and walked. No one had cars, and the workmen had already cycled to their factory or workshop before I left for school. The roads were more or less abandoned and as safe as houses.

St Margaret's was built in 1840 and during the time I was there it catered for boys aged seven to fifteen; I entered when I was eleven. Two of the classrooms had old, heavy wooden desks: these were Mr Rose's and Mr Chittock's rooms. In Mr Chittock's room the desks were moved aside for assembly. In there, too, was a harmonium that Mr Baldry used to accompany our hymns. In Mr Porter's room the 'desks' were of the bench type: long, tiered writing slopes with bench seats. There was a piano in there that the headmaster used for our singing lessons, which was where I learned my early folk songs. Mr Worsnop's room was in the annexe and had more modern desks. The toilets were outside urinals and us boys created patterns resembling the scenic railway on Great Yarmouth's Pleasure Beach as we peed against the pitch-black wall. When the new block was being built and the old toilets dismantled, we were provided with buckets sited in a narrow alley between the annexe and the back of the head's office and cloakrooms. Mr Baldry's office was no bigger than a store cupboard.

It was here that I was introduced to the classic writers of the day: R.M. Ballantyne, H. Rider Haggard, Charles Dickens, Robert Louis Stevenson, Alexandre Dumas and Sir Walter Scott. In this way *The Coral Island, King Solomon's Mines, Oliver Twist, The Dog Crusoe, Kidnapped, Treasure Island, The Master of Ballantrae, The Black Arrow, Robin Hood, The Three Musketeers, The Lost World, Ivanhoe* and other works of these authors became mine. None of these were children's writers, but they were all that was available in the days before the likes of Roger Lancelyn Green, C.S. Lewis, Roald Dahl, Leon Garfield, J.K. Rowling and J.R.R. Tolkien came along. They were not forced upon us, but the masters watched and noted our interests. It was Mr Porter, affectionately known as Sid, who knowing my interest in the *Sherlock Holmes* stories suggested *Trent's Last Case* as being the classic detective story.

A daily assembly was part of our education and we attended church once a month, as I remember, although the priest who was, I think, the Rev Batterbee visited the school more often. What struck me then was that these men were decent people; they were men who had built their lives on the solid rock rather than the shifting sand. When we left St Margaret's we left with a conscience; we had a sense of right and wrong and we knew about guilt. There was no way that any of us could stray from the paths of righteousness and deceive ourselves into thinking that we had not done so. This did not mean that we were all destined never to make an immoral judgement or never act badly; it did mean that we could not hide from what we had done. It also meant that once convinced of the right road to take, we never doubted ourselves and possessed the courage to continue along that road whatever the cost.

Was it here I acquired the fortitude to lead the schools of which I became headteacher along the roads my staff and I considered right rather than follow the dictums of government and the fashions of my contemporaries? Yes it was here. It was here I became what was termed a maverick and later earned the Ofsted comment 'the headteacher has his own idiosyncratic form of management'. Thanks St Margaret's Church of England School for Boys.

The educational skills we learned were basic: comprehension, grammar, handwriting, and arithmetic were at the core of our curriculum and they were repeated year after year. We learned about the work of people in our community, such as the district nurse, and the key dates of our country's history. As I have said, there were no foreign languages or sciences, but we did learn about hygiene and what constituted a healthy diet. A central source of information was the BBC's radio broadcasts and these were accompanied by a booklet in black and white. I remember quite clearly the picture of a dinner plate – divided, pie graph style – showing a balanced meal: protein, carbohydrate, vitamins and minerals. At the end of each term we were tested on what we had learned; and in the term reproduction was covered (without mentioning either a penis or a vagina) the lowest score in the class was 19 out of 20!

Was it here I learned that the best way to educate children was to capture their interests? Yes, it was here.

In our second year, in Mr Worsnop's class, we had the chance to become gardeners. There was a piece of land behind the wall that bordered the playground, and here we learned all I ever came to know about gardening. We planted, sowed, weeded and harvested. I think we may even have taken some of the produce home. It was practical work and of considerable use to us later in life. It was a most relaxing lesson. He joked about the lack of straightness in our rows of potatoes: "It looks as though you lads are you trying to spell out the name of the school!"

We laughed and he laughed with us. I think Mr Worsnop must have had an allotment of his own because I once met him crossing the Woodbridge Road pushing a wheelbarrow. I was so surprised to see a master actually out of school that I stared open-mouthed. He grinned, wished me good morning and we went our separate ways.

We walked to a lane off the Eastern Counties bus station to take woodwork lessons. I enjoyed these with Mr Rix. Again this was a peaceful and purposeful way to spend a morning. Later in life I regretted that boys were not able to learn cooking skills – this being restricted to the girls at Christchurch Secondary Modern School for Girls – which would have been of far more use; but I did cut excellent mortice and tenon joints and produced a decent enough stool.

It was across the girls' playground we were forced to march at lunchtime, since St Margaret's had no kitchen or canteen of its own. This was always a bit of a nightmare, especially as we got older and were still forced to wear shorts and suffer short-back-and-sides haircuts. It was considered that we might become teddy boys if we were allowed long trousers and long hair: more about this in the next chapter. The girls, of course, had lovely hair: flowing manes of unbridled sensuality. Incurably self-conscious at 13, we were obliged to suffer their comments on our legs and haircuts as we walked to lunch.

We wrote with steel nib pens, and the masters, although obsessive about neatness and accuracy of style, were reluctant to replace a bent nib. I can remember them twisting and pressing and forcing them against the metal struts of the desks until they returned to a useable shape rather than give us a new one. Ink adorned our fingers; try as we might to shake off the surplus when we withdrew the pen from the well. The writing slopes had these spaced along their further edge, and each inkwell was linked by a shallow runnel in which we lodged our pens and pencils. Blotting paper was also of a premium and used until the rough, white paper was blue. The important job of ink monitor was now added to that of milk monitor. The ink monitors carried in a tray containing a large number of inkwells, and they placed these in the hole provided on the writing slope. This needed a steady hand because they also had to top up the empty wells from a jug with a narrow spout. Spud Kenny and Robert Howes often got this job: they were both good footballers and probably possessed a well-developed sense of balance. I cannot recall them ever spilling a drop of ink.

The masters wrote with chalk on a blackboard that rested on an easel. Posters and film strips were the only visual aids: the school did not even possess an overhead projector. Their teaching skills rested hugely on the way they presented their subject through talking. Enthusiasm was always apparent and always the key to holding our interest over a lesson running for an hour or so. In this way, the masters were able to pass on their own passions: their keenness for a particular subject ignited our own.

Two horrors of our school days were the Nit Nurse and the Dentist (excuse the capitals!). The nit nurse would arrive at the first sight of any infestation and class by class we would be marched to the medical room where she would examine our heads with a fine nit comb and hard fingers. I don't recall ever having nits and so was spared the usual medications but my mother would go through my scalp every night 'just in case'. She, too, had a nit comb – fine-toothed and double-edged – with which she would search, minutely, for the sign of any invader. I can still feel the pain as hair was tugged away from my scalp, from around my ears and the base of the neck as the comb dug in.

I never avoided the dentist in the same way. The school dentist would visit and a note would be sent home if you needed treatment. At the appointed time, we arrived at Elm

Street Clinic in the centre of Ipswich. Bottle green walls below and dull cream walls above the dado rail led you to the waiting room where hard benches were waiting. The smell in the dentist's surgery was all rubber and gas. A red, rubber bib – hard and inflexible – was tied round your neck and a black rubber gas mask was thrust over your mouth. You breathed in the sickening gas until overcome by unconsciousness. When you woke, there was blood everywhere: in your mouth, on the bib, dribbling over your chin. The 'nurse' – I use that word in the loosest possible sense – walked you over to a metal sluice where she filled an iron mug, which was chained to the wall, with cold water and invited you to swill out your mouth. The blood churning around in your mouth was now diluted and spat into the sluice. In a dazed state, a state in which you were unfit to walk home, the nurse handed you over to your mother. There were no treats afterwards, and with cavities gaping in your mouth a 'treat' would have been anything but a pleasure. They didn't use anaesthetics in those days or consider fillings: anaesthetics and fillings were for the rich.

Games were played on a field somewhere along the Woodbridge Road. I forget where although I walked the distance, which must have been a couple of miles each way, many times. My own dislike of winter sports was not diminished by those we experienced at St Margaret's, which were football and hockey. One or two friends of a similar disposition and I would time our walk in such a way that the games session was more or less over by the time we arrived. The masters knew what we were up to and, generally, turned a blind eye. Occasionally, seeing us arrive so late, they were obliged to do something by way of punishment. This was usually something that would raise a laugh rather than inflict any anguish. Once I was obliged to cut the grass and was quite excited by the prospect until Mr Worsnop, known affectionately as Dickie although his name was actually Robert, handed me a pair of nail scissors. His strategy raised a laugh all round, made the point that the masters could not condone our actions and did me no harm: I suppose I must have cut a square foot at the most.

In summer, it was different: summer meant cricket. If lucky enough to be on the batting side it involved and hour or so stretched out on the grass, listening to the chirping of birds and soaking up the sunshine; if on the fielding side, it meant opting to play long stop because a good wicketkeeper brought about an easy game and time to think.

The other summer activity was swimming, which took place in near freezing water at the open-air Broom Hill swimming pool. Again, this meant a long walk across town and back to school, but once you could swim it was fun. The main teaching technique was a lasso under the arms, whereby the master hauled you in and prevented you sinking while you practised the strokes. I took two summers to learn because so much of the time was spent in fighting off the cold, but once I had mastered the skill I indulged it with fervour. The worst part was the changing rooms: open to the cold with a sheet of sodden canvas attempting to close the doorway.

Corporal punishment has been grossly misrepresented. I witnessed nothing even remotely approaching the general view while I was at St Margaret's. Certainly the cane, the slipper and the stick were used but never in the way stated: wielded to inflict pain by sadistic masters. I never felt demeaned, abused or even punished.

In one instance, I had made a derogatory comment at the back of the class and Mr Rose, affectionately known as Charlie, tapped my backside with a slipper: this gained a laugh from the rest of the class, particularly since my comment related to sports and Charlie chose to use one half of a pair of running spikes.

In another incident, I was caned for attacking a fourth year (14–15 year old) when he went for a friend of mine. The headmaster, affectionately known as Basher Baldry, administered the punishment swiftly, without rancour and with regret.

The third incident I can recall concerned a lifelong friend of mine, Mike Perry. Dickie Worsnop was reading *King Solomon's*

Mines to us when Mike must have said something out of turn. He was asked to step to the front and bend over Dickie's legs, which were stretched out in front of him and resting on a desk while he read. This, itself, caused a laugh and when the already cracked stick broke the whole class, including Mike, was in uproar. Dickie caught on to the humour and asked Mike to pass him the blackboard pointer.

The whole essence of corporal punishment was that it was a symbol stating that certain kinds of misbehaviour were unacceptable. It drew a line under the incident and was always accompanied by good humour all round.

We never mentioned these incidents to our parents, naturally. I know mine would not have given me a wallop to accompany the teacher's reprimand, but they would certainly have disapproved of me far more strenuously than the teacher had done.

I've no regrets that it stopped and it would certainly have been totally unacceptable with girls of any age, but with the boys I knew it did no harm at all.

St Margaret's was a small school and so we all tended to know one another. The school had no catchment area as such, although many children local to the school were accepted, but it was a state school funded through the Local Education Authority. I think the only people guaranteed places were the sons of clergy in the town, and two of these were my friends, Christopher Pritchard, whose father was a vicar and Christopher Woolnough whose father was his curate. The former introduced me to the *Bulldog Drummond* stories by Sapper and the latter to the *Jennings and Darbishire* books by Anthony Buckeridge. I liked the Drummond stories and read most if not all of them, but disliked the first Jennings book, *Jennings goes to School*, and read no more. The fifth book in the Drummond series, *The Female of the Species*, led me on to read Rudyard Kipling's books after I had searched for the poem that gave the book its title. It was quite typical of how reading one book leads on to another quite different in character and quality.

I think my dislike of the *Jennings* books stemmed from the fact that the children portrayed were ostentatiously posh, rather like Enid Blyton's *Famous Five*. They reminded me of the ones who waited outside the posh teashop on the corner of Soane Street: those from the Ipswich High School with the wide-brimmed hats who said things like "Shut your cakehole" in loud voices when they meant "Shut your mouth". We were all aware of the class system in the 50s. It never occurred to me at the time that Drummond with his hatred of Jews, Germans and other foreigners was Sapper's idea of an English gentleman: a jingo imperialist and a racist!

The masters attempted to influence us in their own way. Keith Chittock invited us round to his home, which was a small terraced house situated off the Norwich Road. His lovely wife served us drinks and snacks, and he showed us his collection of books and talked. Never before in my life had I seen rooms where bookshelves reached from floor to ceiling. It was another world, and I think Mr Chittock realised that fact. He talked of things never mentioned at home: philosophy, theatre and opera. He knew we were, in the main, from working class stock and realised our minds needed opening up to possibilities outside our daily experience. He was right. When we moved house in 1957, my father allowed us to have a television set. There were only two channels, as I remember: BBC 1 and ITV. Should anything of an operatic nature appear on either channel, my mother would immediately switch over to the other.

"We don't want to watch that rubbish," she would say.

Similarly, we had never been to the Ipswich Theatre in Tower Street, although for the first two years I walked past it on the way to school each day.

Teachers in those days tended to be from the middle classes and their range of interests had been widened by their own upbringing and education. Every one of them would have been a grammar school boy. When I left school at fifteen my horizons had been widened: although I had no idea what I might do, I no longer saw my working life necessarily centred in an Ipswich factory or workshop.

As we neared the end of our time at the school, the headmaster, Mr Baldry, invited several of us to his house. Once again his wife offered us drink and cakes. Ostensibly, we were there to help him garden – and I remember spoiling one of his borders – but really he wanted to open our minds to the possibility of continuing our education. He had already advised us not to switch to the grammar school when we had the chance at 13.

"You will be two years behind the others," he said, "and have a lot of catching up to do."

He had been right: it would have been a long haul coming from two year's behind on a foreign language and three sciences.

What he must have known but we did not was that the Ipswich Civic College was to open its doors when we left school at fifteen and that this would give us a better chance of success. He was right. In 1959, at the age of 15, I left St Margaret's and went to the School of Commerce and General Studies, which was one part of what was to become the Ipswich Civic College. There the teachers I met showed immense understanding of our vastly disparate backgrounds and were to change my life and my view of the world forever.

What do I owe them? Just about everything.

Chapter 7
Playing Out and Pastimes

We were free in those days: freer than any child living in the modern world can begin to imagine. Quite literally, my mother would pack me a lunch and say: "Make sure you're back for tea."

Tea being the meal we would have when my father arrived home from work on such a day.

Off we would go, at first to Bourne Park, which must have been a couple of miles away, and then further afield to Belstead Brook or Gypswick Park or Freston Shore along the Strand. What age I was when these jaunts began I cannot remember, but certainly Bourne Park was one of our destinations from an early age.

It possessed a wonderful playground with a slide, a roundabout, a witch's hat, a seesaw, swings and a large attraction consisting of a long seat that could accommodate many children. This seat had handles to grip and the device swung backwards and forward between two iron arches. The end seats also had iron backs. Once I saw a girl from a street near our home caught a glancing blow with this seat back. It knocked her down and blood was everywhere. The park attendant who had his own lodge on the grounds looked after her, and by the evening she was on her feet and running around the neighbourhood.

Further into the park a stream flowed. We would dam this with sticks and mud, not realising that it ran through the field where a farmer pastured his cows.

Further still and we came to a wood where the current serial from Saturday morning pictures was enacted: *Rocket Man, Flash Gordon, The Lone Ranger* and *Zorro* all faced their adversaries in the little wood on Bourne Park. Later still, when we were allowed to go to the afternoon pictures, *Tarzan of the Apes, Davy Crockett,* who was *King of the Wild Frontier* and *Sinbad,* fresh from his *Seventh Voyage,* joined our heroes in their battles against the bad guys.

These adventures lived in our imaginations long after the day had come to a close and we were home. In bed at night I would tremble with the memory of hiding behind a tree, still as death, my heart filled with the fear of discovery as an enemy passed by, gun in hand, seeking me out. I was staring him in the face but still he couldn't see me; the secret was to remain motionless, scarcely able to breathe, and become as one with the tree. There were wild chases, too, of course: branches crashing aside, twigs snapping, brambles scoring your legs, bruises and blood everywhere. And there were trees to climb! I've never had a head for heights, but trees were fine: clutching the rough bark, keeping a thick branch between your legs seemed to defy the distance you were from the ground.

We kept together and looked out for each other. No one was expected to wander off or go home alone. If my friend's sisters came we played on the playground; if we had new guns or swords then they were not welcome that day because we would be off to the wood. Some of us were friends at school, while most were from the neighbourhood. It was a long trek down the Wherstead Road to Bourne Park, but we knew a shortcut under the railway bridge and along by the sports ground. Walking there, you could see the trains whistle by, bursting with steam and smoke.

I can only recall only one accident, and that occurred because Patrick did not stay with us and paid with his life. Patrick was a trainspotter, keen as mustard on ticking off the numbers in his book. He told his mother that he was coming with us to Bourne Park but went, instead, in the other direction. On the way to Gypswick Park there was a road bridge over a railway line; it was a wide road leading to the station and the line was fenced off with those high, spiked railings. What actually happened remains the stuff of gossip: we children never did discover the truth. All we saw was the relief on our mothers' faces when we returned home that afternoon; all we sensed was the pall of sadness hanging over the streets. News had preceded us that Patrick had been killed. It was said that while he was standing on the bridge looking down at the line a wheel came off a bus and ran into him. Whether his death happened like this or whether he was, in fact, hit by a runaway bus we were never told. Others said that the wheel had forced him onto the spikes, but I doubted this even at the time because it sounded like genuine gossip – *the sort that revels in speculation, placing the gossiper at the centre of attention.*

He had lived just across the back alley from us and was a good friend of mine, and I can see his face, even now, with its freckles and snub nose and the mop of curly, unruly hair and his intense eyes full of anticipation. Although I can see him now, Patrick disappeared from our lives quickly then. The next day we were playing out as usual.

Richard Dix was a year younger than me but he was probably the closest friend I had in those days. Together with Norman 'Nobby' Fayers and the Sallows boys, Royston and Raymond, Dixie formed our gang. He lived on Vaughan Street just round the corner from Turin Street; his house was on one side of a wide, gravelled alleyway and the Sallows house was on the other. We often played in his garden or that of the Sallows. Dixie's dad had an old workshop; it seemed to grow out of the back of their house, linked to it by the toilet and the coal cellar. I am sure there was a covered way from the back door to the workshop. The workshop, itself, had no door but a large sheet of heavy canvas closed it off from the outside world.

It was there in the workshop, surrounded by tools, that we played out the initiation ceremonies necessary to become a member of the gang. At one time, we were called The Black

Hand Gang, but this did change over the years, as did the rituals of membership. One of these was the Chinese Burn, which involved a senior gang member taking the skin of your wrist in both hands and turning it in opposite directions at the same time; this produces a burning sensation and a degree of pain. Only those who did not cry out were allowed in the gang. Another, less painful, ceremony involved holding your breathe for more than two minutes. Here it was the ritualistic timing by a senior gang member that was the key: the initiate could not know how much longer he would have to go without breathing. He was in the hands of his leader. A third initiation was snuffing out a lighted match. The slower you were able to do this, the tougher you were perceived to be; only a real sap would snuff the match quickly. I developed a variation on this ritual, whereby you put the lighted match in your mouth, removed it still alight and then replaced it in the mouth before blowing out the smoke. *Even now, I fear retribution for revealing these secret ceremonies.*

Gang members were given a badge and a membership card. I do not remember if this was signed in your own blood, but it might have been. In the case of The Black Hand Gang a full hand print was certainly involved. The badges and cards were, I believe, designed by Nobby, although I had a hand in the membership cards. The badges were usually made from stiff card and secured by a safety pin taped to the back. The wording on the cards was based on those we found in comics.

As far as I know, I have been a member of both the Tarzan Club and the Dennis the Menace Club for the best part of sixty years – possibly longer. I came across my badges when my own sons were children, although they seem to have disappeared since that time.

Your gang determined your legitimate territory in the neighbourhood. Ours stretched about half-way along Turin Street, up Vaughan Street as far as Littles Crescent, along Pauline Street (but carefully), through the wide alleyway by Dixie's house and so through the narrow alleyway to Austin

Street (but with a weather eye over your shoulder). Further afield, we ventured down to the docks and along Wherstead Road as far as Bourne Park in one direction and Stoke Bridge in the other.

Further afield did not seem to trouble other gangs: it was the immediate neighbourhood where territory was at a premium. If ever we reached Littles Crescent, which was about 150 yards from Dixie's front door, a rival gang, led by the redoubtable Janet Ostler, always seemed to appear and challenge us to invade their territory. Janet was in my class at school but we never ventured near where she and her friends lived socially. Austin Street kept our nerves on edge because a big lad seemed to dominate the place. He must have been at secondary school when we were still at Luther Road, and he didn't look the kind of person you'd want to challenge.

But there was the temptation of the empty house. This stood at the end of the street opposite a piece of brick-laden wasteland that we believed had suffered bombing during the war. *I have no idea whether or not this was true.* The house was boarded up, of course, but someone, probably boys, had forced an entry. Easing out the planks that covered one of the side windows we were able to gain access. The nails squealed against the stupidity of our intentions, just as our mothers had warned us never to go inside 'because you'll be hit by falling bricks'. It was a dare. We paused at the gaping window, afraid to enter and afraid to dither. Eventually, Dixie, always impetuous, clambered over the broken sill and we followed. Two fears prevailed: the first was that the big kid would nail back the planking and the second was that those bricks would begin falling. Neither eventuality happened. The floors had fallen through to the ground, so that we stared across mounds of brick rubble, and nesting birds flew out through the open roof. We clambered about a bit, moving bricks and fallen rafters, sorting among fag packets no doubt left by the big kid and his mates. But we had dared and conquered our fears.

Was this where I learned to value comradeship in the face of adversity? Was this where I began to learn the value of trusting those around me who shared my fears? Probably, but I cannot be sure.

On one such venture into unchartered territory, I came a cropper. We were returning home through the narrow alleyway that led to the back of Dixie's house and the house of the Sallows boys. I forget why, but we suddenly became aware that someone, a man whose back gate opened onto the alleyway, was waiting for us. He had been cheeked; we were aware of this fact, but how I do not remember. It was apparent that he was waiting for us. We could have avoided the alleyway and simply walked round by the road that led past Uncle Tom's Cabin, but this was not considered as an option. I suppose we could have simply strolled up the alleyway, but such cool was beyond us at that time in our lives. The only way forward was to make a dash. I had reason to believe that it was Raymond Sallows who had cheeked the man, but I do not know that for certain. To his credit, however, Raymond, who was younger than both Dixie and me, opted to make the first run. He passed the gate and reached home base. Emboldened by his luck I made the second run, but unsuccessfully. As I passed the man's gate it opened and I felt a pain shoot through my upper arm. He had me gripped by the elbow and biceps. He was very angry and demanded to know where I lived. I said that I had not cheeked him, but he was insistent and marched me back home. The pain in my arm increased as we walked. My mother answered the door, listened to the man's explosive protests and asked me if I was the one who had cheeked him. I answered that I wasn't. The inevitable question arrived, but I refused to give a name. I wasn't sure, anyway, but even if I had been I would not have split on Raymond. In the end my mother told the man to clear off, and the matter died a natural death. I probably told my mother who I thought it was but she took the matter no further.

Today, of course, the man may have been reported to the police and, possibly, charged with the assault of which he was, patently, guilty. Children may be cheeky, but that doesn't give you or anyone else the right to assault them.

The police were held in awe as figures of authority; but the ones we met were kindly enough and men of discretion. I have said that our territory extended as far as halfway along our back alley. Beyond this point there was a family called the Haggars. We rarely passed their back gate, preferring to reach Kenyon Street along Turin Street or Pauline Street. Bordering Kenyon Street were the almshouses, and through the almshouses was a shortcut to Station Street, which led to school. Cutting through the grounds of the almshouses was always a dare; once or twice it had been done, but always with a feeling of regret because none of us had any desire to upset the tenants. One day we were sitting on the wall of the almshouses contemplating the drop of about six feet to their private grounds. None of us had any intention of jumping; we were just talking when a copper approached. He smiled in the way that neighbourhood coppers always smiled, letting us know that he knew what we thinking and planning: only we had no scheme in mind. As he talked to us, I glanced over my shoulder. The Haggars were standing at the end of the alleyway: mother, two of the children and the grandmother. It was immediately apparent that they had something to do with the arrival of the copper or that he had been talking to them, unnoticed by us, and my next thought was that there had been complaints and that we were suspected. It was also clear that the Haggars wanted this to be the accepted version of the truth, and that the only reason they could possibly have for doing so was that their own children had been the ones responsible for the offence. After his friendly chat to us, during which he took down our names and addresses in his notebook, the copper waved us on our way, which was along Turin Street towards home, and he strolled back to the Haggars.

I was overwhelmed with a sense of unfairness. We'd done nothing wrong and had said so, and yet I had the feeling that the Haggars word had been taken against our own. I was angry, but unable to say anything. *Was this where I gained a sense of the helplessness of children in an adults' world? Was this where the need to listen rather than judge was born? I don't know. What I do know is that children have a deep respect for fairness: to be accused of something they haven't done cuts to the bone. If you listen, you will generally get the truth.*

The Strand, which runs from just past the pub that was called The Ostrich in my boyhood to Freston Shore, is a long stretch of footpath that snakes its way alongside the River Orwell. I think we must have been at least 11 years old before our mothers allowed us to wander this far from home and into an area of potential danger. It was a long summer's day that led to the sandy beach with the little stream that flowed down to the sea through the wood. Dead branches were a highlight because they could be dragged across the sand and stockades could be made. Here, *Treasure Island* would come to life. I could not swim at this time but remember splashing around in the water that lapped shallowly on the beach. We had pen-knives and made swords and shaped twigs into imaginary guns. There were no grown-ups, see, and so our imaginations could run wild, unhindered by comments or inappropriate laughter at our antics.

Within our territory, we were free on the streets. I recall having *Dan Dare's* ray gun – bought by my mother, I believe. It was black with a series of circles at the end of the barrel; these decreased in size from the one at the centre. I was *Dan Dare* that day and in a moment of leadership generosity I loaned it to Raymond Sallows, who was Digby, ordering him to pursue the Mekon's green henchmen along Turin Street. He was off like a hare, tore up Kenyon Street and returned via either the back alley or Pauline Street. On the way, he had dropped the gun, which had broken in half along the central join. Raymond was distressed, and I suppose I must have been less than delighted, but I could see that it was an accident and that nothing could be achieved by falling out with my friend. I reassured him and repaired the gun easily with a couple of elastic bands, one round the barrel and another round the handle.

No one wanted to play the baddies – whether it was Cowboys and Indians or Radar Men from The Moon – and, somehow, we always managed to avoid this happening. The baddies were there, fearful as ever, but they existed only in our imaginations. We shot them down and they stayed down; but if one of us got shot we writhed around for a while on the pavement or the road and then were, magically, 'better'. Up we got and carried on with the game.

At the very edge of our territory, part way along Pauline Street, lived a witch. There was no doubt about this being true. She lived in a house next to a side alley and the walls were painted black. She had black hair and a hooked nose, and the hair was pulled tightly back into a bun. She reminded us of the witch in *Rupert in Trouble Again*: the one who had him hauled up in the cage to hang forever from the castle wall.

The witch and dwarf at a long rope
To pull the cage up strain;
They fasten it securely so
It won't come down again.

But ere they left the witch called out
To him in mocking glee:
"Now, Little Bear, escape from there,
And – if you can – you're free."

Whenever we saw her, the witch was putting out her milk bottles by the front doorstep or shaking rugs over her back fence. She would glance at us, lowering her head and watching under her eyebrows. One dare was to run along the side passage by her house; another was far more risky. The passageway was narrow and it was possible by placing one foot on the neighbour's wall and the other on the witch's black wall to manoeuvre oneself up above the passage. Rubber soles gave a good grip and so, inch by inch, he who took the dare could work his way to the rooftops. I suppose if one of us had ever fallen we would have broken both legs, but our fear resided more in what would happen if the witch came out and found us straddled

"And to give you courage, Little Bear,
I'll tell you, waiting near
Are friends who've come to rescue you
And take you away from here."

And friends were always waiting! The excitement of these stories lay in the question as to what you would do if you found yourself in the same predicament as Rupert.

Belstead Brook in the 1950s was part of the countryside surrounding Ipswich. Beyond Austin Street and up past St Mary at Stoke Church (where my mother and her sisters were married and my sister, Linda, and I were christened), we came to the Belstead Road and the brook. This was a clear-running stream that passed under a little bridge. Around us would be cows in their pastures; these were water meadows where the only screeching came from us and the jays. I do not think we made too much noise by the little bridge because the tranquillity of the place engulfed us; it was the feeling of peacefulness in an already quiet world that was the attraction of the brook. I remember the alders overhanging the water, wagtails perched on stones and dipping their beaks, the sunlight twinkling on the stream through the leaves and the feel of the current through my toes. *Was it this image of the countryside that attracted me to buy my first classical recording: a Music For Pleasure version of The Engima Variations that had just such a picture on the sleeve?*

Girls played little or no part in any of these adventures, but there were exceptions. Dixie's twin sisters were one: Dorothy ('Doff') and Pam would sometimes tag along. The other was Nobby's sister, whose name I forget but who was fond of putting on plays and shows in their back garden, which opened onto the passageway separating their garden from Dixie's. She would summon us to attend and line us up on the lawn. When we were sitting cross-legged to her satisfaction, the show would start. A sheet was strung on a linen line in front of the audience, and she and her friends would appear, acting out a play they had devised or singing a few songs popular at the time such as *How Much Is That Doggy In The Window* or *Pink Toothbrush, Blue Toothbrush*. I have a vague memory that Nobby's mum would bring us squash and cupcakes at the end of the performance.

Where girls did have a huge influence was in the organising of games on the street. They would appear suddenly, often with amazingly long **skipping** ropes that would be strung out across the road. (Remember there were no cars to speak of back then.) One girl would stand on one pavement and a second on the other. Sometimes, we would be asked to help turn the rope. One girl would then jump into the rope and proceed to skip. She would be followed by another and then another and so on until there would be up to half-a-dozen skipping in the rope, which struck the road with a swish and a crack. They were extremely clever at skipping, whether alone or in a group. Sometimes they skipped to nursery rhymes, but at others they used special skipping rhymes that contained key words: these indicated to other girls when to enter the rope and when to leave.

> *I love coffee, I love tea*
> *I want* (name of a friend) *to jump in with me*
> *Two little dickie birds sitting on the wall*
> (two more jump in)
> *Fly away Peter, fly away Paul*
> (two jump out)
> *Don't you come back 'til your birthday's called.*
> *January, February ... and so on to December*
> (skippers enter as birthday is called)
> *Now fly away, fly away, fly away all*
> (skippers leave in order)

Girls were fond of **handstands**. They did these individually and usually against a wall. As their legs went up and their feet rested on the wall, their dresses would fall down over their faces, showing off their navy blue knickers. All girls seemed to wear such knickers. A variation of this was **cartwheels**. However good boys were at this activity, they always seemed to lack the elegance of the girls. Some would perform several in sequence, showing off their knickers each time. If anyone mentioned the word 'knickers' everyone would laugh, but the sight of them brought no merriment or even a ribald comment. As the girls got older they tucked their dresses into the leg elastic of their knickers so that their underwear could not be seen. **Leapfrog** was another popular athletic game that depended on the sturdiness of the frogs. Girls played this with equal skill and strength. Once it was underway, with each frog having no further leapers to come, the frog would then follow on. In this way the game could continue along one side of a street. It was also possible for children of varying ages to be involved: all that was needed was the strength to maintain a solid frog and the agility to leap.

Girls were also good at **juggling**. They did this with rubber balls or old tennis balls and many could keep several on the move at one time. The balls were sometimes juggled in the air but as often as not they were juggled against a wall or even downwards onto the pavement.

Left to themselves, the girls played a game called **cat's cradle**. I never got the hang of this and would stare in amazement as they looped and twisted a piece of string or an elastic band round their fingers making intricate patterns. Sometimes two of them would share the cradle passing it from one to the other without dropping a loop.

Hopscotch I enjoyed thoroughly. Once again the girls organised us boys into playing this game as they did with another favourite, **What's the time Mr Wolf?** Once either of these games was underway, other children not normally seen in our territory would join in, and I can recall twenty or more of us involved, our stomachs churning with terror at being caught by the wolf. Hopscotch would be played on the pavement and we always got into trouble for chalking the numbers on the paving slabs, which were ideal for the game because of the alternate way in which they were laid. 'What's the time, Mr Wolf' would be played across the street with the wolf facing the house wall on one side and the rest of us advancing from the other.

It or **tag** was probably the most widespread game and often sprang up from nowhere: the sudden appearance of a new child would bring it into action. There were many variations. You could become 'It' simply by being touched; in other versions, the chaser had to lift you from the ground. In a team version, you had to sit down if touched until the 'It' team had caught everyone in yours; you could be released by another member of your team who was untouched. It was possible to avoid being touched by removing your feet from the ground; this could be achieved by leaping onto someone's doorstep or hanging from a windowsill.

Getting dirty and ruining your clothes was never a problem because the clothes you wore were old school ones that no longer fitted you or hand-me-downs from a relative. No one bought new clothes for playing out.

Some games were seasonal, of course: the obvious one being **conkers**. There were various theories about increasing the strength of your conker: the most prevalent was that soaking it in vinegar did the trick. One or two boys kept a champion conker from year to year, but really there was nothing to beat a large, fresh one. A conker was always referred to by the number of others it had smashed: so it was a 'one-er' or a 'two-er' and so on. If you managed to smash a 'two-er', yours became a 'three-er'. I once had a friend in tears because I smashed his 'six-er'. A prize conker became a treasured possession, and once it became a real champion was often kept safely in a tin to fight no more.

Very few of these games required the purchase of special equipment: every item needed was usually homemade. This included skipping ropes, which were often pieces of old linen line. Even **five-stones** was played with stones found at the side of the road, although a more sophisticated version called **jacks** was played with those spiky metal objects bought in toy or joke shops. Another exception was **yo-yo**, which reared its head from time to time.

Girls played with yo-yos but conkers and five stones were, generally, boys' games, although my sister insists that she and a friend were adepts. Conkers could be quite painful if the opponent's conker struck your hand. Other rough games from which girls tended to steer clear were **British bulldog** and **bumps** (reserved for your birthday and highly dangerous). They also never got involved in **marbles**. Why I do not know. Boys would keep marbles from year to year (I still have mine) and some became very precious. You would usually play them on the clear understanding that if your opponent won they chose another marble as their prize: no one ever gave away their best marble. And I never saw a girl allow herself to get involved in **Ginger's Knock!**

There were rainy days, of course, when you sat staring out of the living room window onto the back garden: rainy days and Sundays. We never went to church as a family, but, even so, we were never allowed to play out on a Sunday. Only 'common' families allowed their children to play in the street on a Sunday and they were not many of those 'over Stoke'.

However, I can never remember being bored. I think most of us had hobbies, pastimes or interests. Stamp collecting was a widespread hobby, and I was very lucky because my father was in the Royal Navy and brought home stamps from abroad. I still have the album. *I do not think anyone collected stamps in the serious anticipation that one of them might, in the future, be worth a fortune; they were collected because collecting is addictive.* It was wonderful to open the blue, Stanley Gibbons album and just take in the beauty of the stamps. English stamps were rather plain, on the whole, with the King or Queen's face dominating, but foreign stamps were very attractive, featuring sporting events and national occasions as well as views of the country from which they came.

My father was on the Royal Yacht and during the world tour of 1956 visited Australia. As a result of this he acquired for me stamps of the Melbourne Olympic Games. They were stuck on an envelope and date stamped, and my favourite was one of a swimmer, right arm stretched from the water, doing the front crawl. He also visited Tristan da Cunha and I have a set of stamps from the island; this was before the volcanic eruption made it uninhabitable for some time. When the islanders evacuated, the priest destroyed the printing press and so any stamps prior to that time are now unusual but not rare.

I was bought a Meccano set at an early age but with the exception of a huge, working windmill my dad helped me make I did little with it. My parents thought that a big set would offer me more opportunities, but because it was big it had to be second hand and came soiled and rusty in places. I thought at the time I would have preferred a smaller set even, or especially, if this allowed me to create only one or two decent models. *Was it from this experience I learned that creative endeavours should be within the capabilities of the child? Yes it was, and this knowledge served me in good stead as a father and as a teacher. Keep challenges within the range of the possible.*

A craze of the time was the making of crystal sets, and I came across a model for one in one of my annuals, probably the *Eagle Annual*. Several of my friends were taken up with the same desire to make one, and one of us, probably Nobby Fayers, heard of a little shop along the Norwich Road, just past St Matthew's Swimming Baths, that supplied the parts. The man, clearly amused by the earnestness of youngsters, was very helpful and I left with the necessary components. Putting them together was another matter, but my father made me a base, a front board for the dial and a small side board for the various connections. It was a beautiful piece of woodwork and I kept it for years. He also fashioned a cylinder with two circles of plywood and a Vim carton. "Tickling the whisker" was the expression used to tune the crystal to the right position, and this seemed to amuse Dad who laughed unmercifully as I tried to contact a radio station. We juggled with the aerial, running it through the back window of the living room, but to no avail. I never did receive a signal.

Annuals were a great consolation during my childhood. We had the radio but there was no television and so reading was a major source of amusement and education. The *Rupert Annual* always contained something to make from paper: a plane, a boat, a jack-in-the-box. *Later, I was to make the boat full size for a school play.* There was also the *Buffalo Bill Annual*, which was stacked full of information about the Wild West as well as more things to make, including the Red Indians' tepee, tomahawk and bow and arrow. Two great favourites of mine were a *Cinema Annual*, which narrated the story of films I had never seen and had photos from the films, and a *Bertram Mills Circus* book. I pored over this for years until it became quite dog-eared. In both these books the attraction was in the glamour of the actors and actresses and the circus performers.

Other annuals I remember were the *Beano*, the *Dandy* and, as I recall, the *Tiger*, where our comic heroes lived again: Lord Snooty and his Pals, Desperate Dan with his cow pies, Dennis being slippered by his dad, the Bash Street Kids and the boxer, Biff Bailey. We spent hours reading these annuals over and over again.

Many of the stories and much of the information I gleaned from these annuals are still with me today. I recall Luke, Jeff Arnold's 'sidekick' from the Eagle apparently lassoing a train to a standstill and remember Jeff's explanation. Luke was renowned for his 'tall stories' and Jeff's explanation to his questioner showed respect for the old man's feelings about his feat. I learned something from that story about respect for the old. I think I could recount the story of Custer's Last Stand as though I was there with Crazy Horse and the Sioux as they charged into the valley and massacred the Seventh Cavalry.

I had a desk in the corner of the living room (it would have been too cold in my bedroom, which was unheated) and there I kept my books and collections. It was a rickety desk made, I think, by a firm called Triang but it occupied me. Inside was a pencil box with a sliding lid (made by my father and handed down to my sister, and which she still possesses) and a tin in which I stored real treasures: a champion conker, a small pipe from my Grandad Bathstreet, a catapult, a precious marble, my membership cards and badges for the *Dennis the Menace* and *Tarzan* clubs, a stone with a hole in it found on Felixstowe beach, cigarette and bubble gum cards.

Another pastime was my chemistry set, which comprised test tubes filled with chemicals of various colours. Some of them were really bright. I remember blues, whites and reds in particular. But the set was largely a waste of time. The experiments were printed minutely inside a small unillustrated booklet and they lacked excitement. I was expecting explosions or puffs of smoke, but nothing of the sort occurred.

My Mamod steam engine was a different matter, however: I spent hours and hours playing with it. It consisted of a copper boiler supported by a black frame on a red base. The boiler was filled with water, which was heated by a small burner filled with methylated spirits. When the water was hot enough, steam would issue from the funnel or could be directed via the piston to turn a wheel. In turn, this wheel could be connected by a leather belt to a circular saw or a windmill. Once the piston was oiled and the wheel spun, the saw was able to cut matchsticks and the sails of the windmill turned. I found the combined smells of the methylated spirits and the oil together with the sight of the steam as it spluttered through the piston to be fascinating. *Years later, when I was a teacher, I took my steam engine into class when our children were studying the 1950s.*

With metal, toy soldiers I created battles. With my mother I completed jigsaw puzzles; we spent days putting jigsaw pieces together into a picture. She taught me how to play card games like Patience, Snap, Old Maid and Happy Families; we played dominoes, bingo and draughts with my father and, later, my sister. We had scrapbooks and did tracings. I played with my clockwork train set on the living room floor.

Hours and hours were spent sitting at the table or lying on the floor amusing myself. *I was never interrupted once I began* to play and my imagination was fully engaged. One of my sons, talking about one of his own children, once said to me that his daughter was never alone: there was never a moment when her mobile phone might not ring or the television might not distract her from whatever she was doing at the time. During my childhood, I was fortunate enough to spend hours totally focussed on the job or pleasure in hand. Was this where I learned to concentrate? Oh yes, it was here.

The Rupert Annual that contained the stories Rupert, the Witch and Tabitha and Rupert in Trouble Again, 1950

Chapter 8
Neighbours and the Neighbourhood

Although my mother liked to 'keep herself to herself' we knew many of our neighbours quite well. There was Jack Finch who flew racing pigeons, Mr Stannard who bred rabbits, Mr and Mrs Whales who kept the corner shop, the Jackman boy who always whistled beautifully as he strode along the alley, Mrs Bird who called me a snob, the posh lady directly across the passage who had a graceful Collie and who we tormented with the game Ginger's Knock, Veronica who ate jam sandwiches sitting in the gutter ... and those I have already mentioned: Miss Pullin, the Haggars, the Dix family, the Sallows, the Fayers and the man whose name I did not mention, but who my mother chased with a clothes prop. It was a colourful neighbourhood in many ways.

My parents bought the house for £660 soon after they were married in 1940, as far as I know. Certainly, we returned to it from Scotland in October 1947. They sold it in 1957 for £750 because my father did not believe it morally right to make too much profit. (Their new bungalow cost £2,500 at that time.) It was 'over Stoke', quite near the docks, and was considered a nice house.

The fathers of the children I knew were all working people: craftsmen like my father, factory workers, van drivers, bus conductors, railwaymen and clerks. Judging from my memory of the election posters in windows, I think the neighbourhood was solid Labour. During one political campaign, we children went round the streets singing:

Vote, vote, vote for Mr Stokes
Hit old Ripley in the eye.
If it wasn't for the law
We'd knock him through the floor
Vote, vote, vote for Mr Stokes.

We had no idea who any of these people were, of course, and wished them no harm: I was only six at the time but, anyway, politics was never discussed in our house. *I think the people of Ipswich voted Labour because they believed that it would help to change society for the better, but all I heard at the time were odd comments that came to me at the table, from the armchair and in the street*: the upper classes always take good care of themselves, industry ... too important to be left in private hands, the National Health Service, the rights of employees. It all seemed rather good-natured, and I remember thinking that Mr Stokes ought to be elected because he had the right name for the area.

I learned later that Mr Stokes was Richard Rapier Stokes (known as Dick) and that Mr Ripley was his Conservative opponent in the 1950 general election.

I think the NHS made medicine and doctors more available to people like us, who would not considered, or been able, to pay privately. As I have said, I remember our doctor visiting when I was sick and I was told he recommended lots of rest for my many illnesses. He was not averse to pulling joints into place, I understand, and I can remember friends having stitches in wounds without anaesthetic. If you were ill, you called the doctor. Ours arrived smelling of drink on one occasion and my mother ordered him out of the house, never to return.

The house next to ours was the corner shop owned by Mr and Mrs Whales (the spelling is from memory). They sold groceries, greengroceries, sweets and general food provisions. The door opened onto the actual corner and a bell rang as you entered. The main counter, which was wooden, was to the rear of the shop immediately in front as a customer entered. I have a vague memory of a second counter running along on the right hand side; there seemed to be sacks of items like potatoes in front of this counter. The rear of the shop was dark even when the window was lit on winter evenings. Traditional jars of sweets lined the shelves and these were weighed before being slid into a brown paper bag.

I forget exactly how much pocket money I had but I think it was sixpence a week (2.5p). You could buy a lot of sweets for that amount: four fruit chews could be bought for a penny, and there were bags of sherbet with a stick of liquorice that could be dipped in the bag and the sherbet licked off. Liquorice came in all shapes and sorts; my favourites were the ones you could unfurl and that had an all-sort in the centre.

Once sweet rationing had ended, Mr and Mrs Whales stocked sweets such as Spangles, Bassett's Liquorice Allsorts, Wagon Wheels, Refreshers, Love Hearts and Rowntree's Fruit Gums. A big lure were the bubble gum cards that came in packs of the gum. These had scenes from films, and an album could be purchased to stick them in. I loathed bubble gum but was desperate to collect the whole set of cards, and so I gave the gum to my friends in exchange for any swaps they had: that is, cards of which they had two or more

Mrs Whales was short and plump, and always wore one of these wrap-around pinafores. Mr Whales was tall, with greying, Brylcreemed hair, and he wore the buff coloured overall that seems to have been the uniform of shopkeepers in those days. Since we lived next door, they knew our parents well: Mum would 'pop over the back fence' for odd items after hours.

The lighted window was a magnet for us children at night. We would stand against the sill, leaning on the many small panes of glass and just talk. The shop was open all hours, of course, and the light cast yellow shadows onto the pavement, winter or summer.

It was here I conversed for hours with my first girlfriend. I think she must have been a year or two younger than my 11 or 12 years. She was blonde and what people called 'comely';

she had a pale face with a snub nose and light blue eyes. Her name was Una and she was a foster child. She had been fostered by Patrick's family as a sister for Susan after Patrick was killed. Our relationship consisted of the occasional kiss, an arm round the waist and simply being close. She was far more streetwise than me, and I knew this at the time without understanding why or even having heard of the word 'streetwise'. Her father, she said, had been a naval officer – although whether this was true or not I am unsure – and she had a sister, older than her, who was also fostered. Una was unhappy, and said she preferred the orphanage to the foster home: not that her treatment had been unkind, but she felt she did not belong in the home. In the end, I remember persuading her to write to her sister who duly appeared on the scene and Una vanished from our neighbourhood as suddenly as she had arrived.

It was on this corner of Turin Street and Vaughan Street that the Salvation Army band would stand and play on a Saturday or Sunday morning. We children would sit on our doorsteps or on the kerb, listening and watching. One of the band walked along the street and perhaps knocked on doors (but I am unsure of this fact), rattling a wooden collection box. I loved the tunes: they were inspiring. At Christmas time, the band would play carols. We were never disturbed by our parents, and many of the grown-ups living on the street would come out and join us to listen. After they had played for a while, the Salvation Army would move on to the corner of the next street, Pauline Street, and we would follow but never ventured outside our territory.

Other visitors to the street included the ice cream van with its peal of bells, the rag and bone man and the fishmonger.

The rag and bone man had a horse and cart, exactly like the one shown in the television series, *Steptoe and Son*, broadcast in 1962. He had a cry that was indistinguishable from a long grunt but presumably called for our junk. When this was brought out he tossed it onto his cart, clicked his teeth and slapped the reins on the horse's back to move it on. The horse was an old-looking animal of the Suffolk Punch type: huge hooves that rattled on the road and long matted mane and tail. It moved slowly with little or no guidance from the man. By the time he had finished his round the cart was full of unwanted items: pipes, battered prams, anything that contained metal. Sometimes we children would wander down to the scrap yard with bits of metal we had found on the dumps and wasteland; it would be weighed and we would be paid accordingly.

The fishmonger rode a bike with a large basket at the front in which he carried shrimps and prawns. It was possible to buy a pint of shrimps, and we children would be sent out with a bowl that he would fill from a pint mug. My mum and I would then peel the shrimps ready for tea, and this was always a treat; we ate them with bread and butter.

Jack Finch's pigeons were flown regularly and because I played with his son, David, I was able to see them at close hand. I was always puzzled by how they could fly into their loft through the opening covered by ropes weighted by a wooden batten, but never fly out. Mr Finch would stand in his garden as they circled round the neighbourhood, the whole flock wheeling together in the sky. When he wanted them back he shook their seeds in a silver tin with blue writing, which I believe had contained powdered milk, until they came. There was magic in this calling: so many birds responding to the soft rattling of a tin and the clicking of his teeth.

Further along the back alleyway lived Mr Stannard, who kept rabbits for their meat and their fur. Meat rationing was still in force until I was 10 and so rabbit was a very acceptable addition to the diet. I cannot ever remember my mother cooking it, but I do recall seeing dozens of rabbits hanging in one of the butcher's shops. Mum did, however, buy a pair of gloves with the softest fur imaginable from Mr Stannard, as well as a pair of mittens for Linda, and I can recall her waiting with great anticipation until Mr Stannard said, "the rabbit was ready". *Strangely, none of this made me realize that the rabbits were killed. I saw them in their hutches, one stacked on top of another so high that they seemed to form the side of a shed; but the fact that they were there to be slaughtered never entered my mind.*

Pubs played no part in our lives: my parents simply did not frequent the locals. There were two of these that I remember: the Eagle Tavern in Bath Street, which was used by my grandparents, and Uncle Tom's Cabin on the corner of Austin Street. I have already said that I once found myself in the pub with my grandad, but how this came about I have no idea because children were not allowed. What usually happened with those people who did 'like a drink' (and that term, itself, was always uttered with the raising of an eyebrow) was that the children were left sitting outside with a glass of lemonade and a packet of Smith's Crisps; these were fascinating as they had a little twist of blue paper inside that contained the salt. It was always exciting to find the bag among the crisps, tipped the salt onto them and give the bag a good shake.

The neighbourhood was served with one telephone box that stood on the corner of Wherstead Road and Purplett Street, which led down to the River Orwell. I believe a post office stood nearby and across the road was the public house called Uncle Tom's Cabin. People would line up to use this telephone, which was housed in a red telephone box. I can recall a queue of people stretching down Purplett Street waiting for someone to finish a call. If it had taken a long time, they would always apologise to the queue and some wit would call out a remark like: "Don't worry, sweetheart, it's just that our house is on fire."

This would always raise a laugh, but there was never any animosity towards the person who had kept everyone waiting. There were two buttons in the telephone box: button A was pressed to connect a call once you had paid and button B was to get your money back if the call was not answered. Since few people had telephones most of these calls must have been of an official nature – doctor, hospital, fire brigade, police – but some must also have been to those lucky relatives who were 'on the phone', judging by the length of time they consumed.

The police, themselves, had a special box – the blue ones that appeared as *Doctor Who's* Tardis in 1963 – but the public were not allowed to use these. One stood just over Stoke Bridge across the road from the docks.

Stoke Bridge was for a while the outer limit of where I could roam, and after I had learned to read at the age of seven it was to become very familiar to me because here was the public library. Remember, we had few books of our own in those days, and so the public library was a major source of our enjoyment and education. There was a notice telling us to be silent and there was no children's corner, but that didn't make the library feel unwelcoming. I think there must have been an area that specialised in children's books because I can remember always making for one particular place; here were both fiction and non-fiction books. I don't remember being able to stay except to browse but we could and did take out six books at a time. Here I expanded my knowledge of the world. The librarian would stamp the book with a return date, take out the small card ticket in the pocket at the front of the book and place this in a similar pocket she had in a narrow, wooden box. I suppose these must have been in date order, otherwise she would have never found them again. *I say 'she' because I do not ever recall seeing a male librarian.*

Across the bridge were the docks proper with their wonderful smell of cereals and grains. Something was milled here: wheat into flour, barley into meal. Sacks were lifted from the ships and disappeared through trapdoors into the lofts of the warehouses, their contents to appear later sliding down shoots and onto lorries. I remember large, flat-bottomed boats with masts and black and red sails.

Further afield still we came to Fore Street and the Fore Street Swimming Baths. Fore Street was in an older part of the town where the buildings were beamed and leaned over onto the street. This was an area of traditional shops: ironmongers and watch repairers are two I remember. I didn't learn to swim until I was 13 and it was soon after this that we moved, and so

I can only think that in the early days, probably from the age of 11, I came here with my friends as a non-swimmer; presumably we splashed about in the shallow end, but the water was hot and steaming and so we enjoyed it.

Further afield meant further into the town. As younger children we had been allowed to wander for several miles in the direction of Bourne Park, but the town must have been seen by our parents, even then, as posing additional hazards. Until I was 11, Christchurch Park must have been the limit of my travels; after I was 11, it was somewhere I passed every day on the way to school. The park contained the Mansion House, which possessed suits of armour and medieval weaponry, but otherwise held no interest for me at that age. The ducks made it worthwhile to carry a bag of stale breadcrumbs. The arboretum was either out of bounds to children or a charge was levied. I forget which sanction applied, but the only time I ever went there was with my Grandad Bathstreet on a Sunday morning. Mum's last reminder was always to be out 'before the park closed'. There were park attendants in those days who kept the louts in order, but there was always the fear that you might be locked in at night. I think I remember a bell being rung about thirty minutes before the gates were locked.

I had a strange experience sometime between the age of seven and 11. As I have said, there were limits to our territory. We rarely ventured the whole way along the back alley as far as the Haggars unless it was with a specific purpose such as visiting Mr Stannard's rabbits. However, one day I must have been wandering along there alone when I was stopped by an older girl. I say older but she cannot, I think, have been more than 12 or 13. She and her mother had arrived on the street a short time before; there was no father apparent. She was taller than me and I recall being aware of this fact quite acutely. I was also aware of a class difference: it was in her manner and her voice. Her hair was wavy and golden brown. She had a soft face and a caressing voice. I am not sure how it happened but I found myself sitting on the seat of the outside toilet undressed to the waist. There was a bowl of warm water placed to hand and the girl was washing my chest and arms very gently in long, slow easy movements. How long this went on I have no idea but it was very pleasant. As she washed me she talked and her voice was easy and soothing. After a while, the toilet door opened and the girl's mother stood watching us. "What are you doing?" she asked.

I have no memory of what the girl said, but there was no anger and no upset in either her manner or that of her mother.

"I think we had better finish now," she said, "and then you can go home."

I noticed a certain anxiety in her tone, as though she wanted the incident closed. After a while, I found myself dressed and walking back along the passageway. Nothing more was ever said either by my mother or the girl's, and I have no recollection of ever seeing her again.

On the whole we were, I think, well-behaved children. Certainly, had it been otherwise and had any bad behaviour been reported home by the school or the police we would have got it in the neck. Our parents would have supported the official view without question. One game we did play, if infrequently, was Ginger's Knock, and our usual victim were the people who lived in the house across the passageway from us. I have no idea why we picked on them: the lady was pleasant and they were the owners of a beautiful collie. I think it was the husband who aroused our antagonism. He was one of those mean-faced men with thinning hair who never smiled at children. Their front door opened onto Vaughan Street rather than Pauline Street and so the dare was to rattle their knocker and run to a hiding place before we were caught. The two obvious hiding places were the low wall at the side of the alleyway by Dixie's house and the narrow passage that ran along by the witch's house on Pauline Street. The first knock was child's play, of course, since the victim was unprepared; but the second and third knocks were undertaken at great risk and timing was critical. Had the man given up and was no longer lurking behind his front door or was he waiting? I can recall watching his angry face as we crouched by Dixie's wall and of us being creased up with laughter. There was no question of this being simply mischievous; we were in no doubt at all that what we were doing was wrong.

I was a year older than Dixie and for that reason and no other there was a sense in which I was the leader of the gang. I never instigated this game but I went along with it, and felt the guilt. I was aware that I should have stopped it before we started. I didn't, and the fault was mine. I couldn't put my exact feelings into words at the time but whenever I thought about the incident years later it taught me that a leader should do just that and never be led.

The Americans were in Britain at that time, and we liked them. How could we not? The Sallows boys had older sisters, and American servicemen would often be seen at their house, standing in the front garden, leaning over the wall, eager to engage us in conversation. We found them to be friendly, and the 'Yanks Go Home' attitude was not something I ever experienced. My mother had a certain reservation, but this was centred on the girls as much as the servicemen: that is all I can say. What struck us as strange were their faces as much as their voices. They looked different and this made us wary. *Looking back now, it seems to me that the ones we saw were of Spanish origin; the nearest faces to theirs I have seen as an adult are Mexicans. Back in the 1950s, they were just strange to behold, in much the same way as someone from China would have seemed odd to us.*

There was, I believe, a wide range of wealth over Stoke. *We were lucky because Dad had a secure job and was well paid; others were not so fortunate.* I was aware of this difference in several ways. People who didn't keep their gardens cultivated and clear of debris were often referred to as 'not having two halfpennies to rub together'; the same recriminations were applied to those with peeling paintwork, un-scrubbed doorsteps, faded curtains or dirty windows. There was an expectation that certain standards were to be maintained at all costs. On the other side of the fence, so to speak, people who maintained a particularly high standard of décor, such as a brass door-knocker, were often referred to as snobs. Even as a child I was aware of a degree of envy where money was concerned; and envy produces judgements. *Is there where I learned to be wary of judgements produced from envy? Yes, it was here because I knew them to be false.*

Croft Street ran parallel with Station Street and somewhere between the two, on the Wherstead Road, was Stoke Baptist Church. Mrs Lewis, who had taught me to read, was the Baptist Minister's wife and it may have been through her that I ended up in the Wolf Cub pack at the Baptist church. Equally, it might have been through her son, David, who was in my class at school. *I have always had a respect for religion: not for its excesses, its pomposity, its lies and its blind eye but for its importance to people on a daily and domestic basis and for the good work churches do in their communities. Was it here that I began to appreciate its value? Yes, it was most certainly here.*

What I began to learn here were moral values based on a Christian way of life. They were not preached, but witnessed in the simple fact that Akela and Bagheera were prepared to give their time to run the pack. I remember being appalled one day when my mother said: "Bagheera! Huh! She's nobody. I went to school with her!"

My mother was wrong to make such a judgement, and I knew it then as clearly as I know it now. The very fact that Bagheera gave her time for us made her somebody very important indeed. It raised her in our eyes as someone to be admired, and we did. My mother's attitude brought into question my respect for her at that time; *but I was a child and had yet to learn about the frailties of human nature.*

I disliked school uniform intensely but did not mind that of the Cubs': the wretched cap could be stuffed in your pocket unless you were on parade and the neckerchief likewise. Besides, I rather liked folding the neckerchief with its alternate yellows and greens; and Mum always ironed it so that it was smooth and immaculate.

The abiding image of Cub packs and Scout troops stems from the usual sneer of the 'pinko-trendy, liberal left' as they deride the "dib-dib-dib" and "Akela we will do our best". But there was a lot more to the organisation. There was order and a patently fair progression through the ranks to become a sixer or seconder, and it was good for the older boys to be responsible for the conduct of six of the younger. For any boy not interested in this kind of thing there were the proficiency badges that capitalised on our likely interests: map reading, book reading, stamp collecting, model making, bird watching ... and so on. I was as lazy in the pack as I was at school, quite content to drift along doing what interested me; and there was no end-of-term or end-of-year report that had to be justified to your father. It took you away from home for one night a week and was the beginning of a sense of freedom for the individual. Provided you worked it ensured success: tying knots, making fires, pitching tents. It was fun: there were always free times to race around the churchyard, organised games in which everyone engaged at their level rather than having to wait to be picked for the team and boisterous versions of street favourites such as British Bulldog.

Later, I was to move on to the Sea Scouts and these were based at the church of St Mary at Stoke. *In the troop there was certainly a greater note of patriotism, but it never verged on the jingoistic and was not politically motivated.* It was run by decent men who thought it quite reasonable to swear allegiance to your monarch, your god, your country and your neighbour: these were promises we had to make. *Again I see the sneers and hear the mocking laughter of the 'I live my life my way by my rules' brigade, but what does that mean except that such people always put themselves before everybody else: the selfish and the purely self-interested.*

I must have been in the Sea Scouts for only two years, from 11 to 13, because I have no memory of travelling back to

Stoke once we moved in 1957, *but they were a formative time in my life*. Activities begun in Cubs continued, but more was expected of us. *We were all beginning the difficult journey into adolescence and whereas every consideration is given now, none was allowed in those days. Adolescence was not seen as a stage between the child and the adult;* we were viewed as simply being awkward.

My two most vivid memories of being in the Scouts are of camp and marching. St George's Day was always wet and cold and these two elements were often whipped up by the wind. Trousers in those days were made of a material called worsted, and we wore our trousers short. We were kept in short trousers as long as possible. I can recall being laughed at by the girls of Christchurch Secondary when I was forced to go to school in them at the age of 13; the scout troop was no different. We waited in foul weather until the scout band had itself in position and then we marched through Ipswich to present our colours, sodden wet and with the worsted trousers rubbing our legs raw as they did every time we went to school.

As a Sea Scout, photographed in our backyard at Turin Street, 1956

Scout camp was most enjoyable. We really did use those skills we had honed to near perfection on troop nights: we chopped branches with axes, we lit fires by rubbing two sticks together, we dug latrines, we pitched our tents, we forded streams, we created bivouacs, we were dropped off to find our way back to camp using map and compass.

I was never old enough to become a patrol leader and was not dismayed, having witnessed how distressed our leader became at camp. I'll call the boy Smith. He can only have been about 15 and carried responsibility for his patrol. One of these was to prepare the meals. I saw him one day, bending over the stew pot, tears streaming from his eyes, being baited by two of his patrol. *Was it then I came to detest louts as much as I do even to this day? Yes, it was then.* I'll call the pair Thomas and Newell. They did nothing to help but sat back laughing as Smithy tried to cook our dinner over a camp fire: laughing and grumbling like spoilt children over the mess he was making of the task, picking constantly at the sight of the stew in the pot.

"Do you want your mum, Smithy!" they sneered, knowing he was homesick. Smithy blushed with embarrassment and his tears ran more freely. They had been goading him all week: the tent was draughty, the ground sheet rucked up, the dining shelter was wobbly. Smithy had suffered enough and he wanted to go home.

"You int crying into our stew are you Smithy?" they continued.

His bloodshot eyes scanned the rest of us and we smiled back what we hoped were smiles of encouragement. I met Thomas at the Ipswich Civic College in 1959. He hadn't changed: once a lout, always a lout. By then he had turned his attention to girls, and his treatment of them was on a par with his treatment of Smithy only now it manifested itself in what is called charm.

What did I learn from that experience? I learned how to deal with louts: make them laughing stocks by delegating them the jobs they'll find difficult. I learned to assess my colleagues:

give the barrack room lawyer types, the know-alls of this world, the research and the presentations. If watching Smithy's distress that day did anything to form my character, it put the iron in my soul.

What both organisations also did was to put me in touch with people who were driven by their religious faith: they didn't put themselves out because they were paid, but because they thought it right. This gave me an admiration for people with faith whether I agreed with them or not, and it's an admiration I still feel strongly.

We were invited to a Baptist baptism. It was a simple church building: stark, straight-backed pews, no decorations, cold and permeated with the mustiness of old books. We sat in the front row and opened before us was what looked like a small swimming pool. It had appeared as if by magic where the floor had once occupied the space. Steps led down and a minister stood at the bottom. Those ready to receive baptism, *and they were all adults because Baptists believe that a person must decide such weighty matters and answer for themselves,* were dressed in what looked like sheets. They were led down into the water and with the minister supporting their head were lowered beneath the surface. It was the first time I had witnessed baptism by total immersion and I was deeply impressed. I recall nothing else of the service: just the faces of those being accepted into the Baptist church.

This then was our neighbourhood and some of my neighbours. Thinking back, I realise what an awful lot it was for a child to take in, but I had the time to do it: to see, to brood, to think, to wander, to wonder and to grow.

Chapter 9
Saturday Morning Pictures and Going Up Town

Going to Saturday morning pictures was one huge step on the road to growing up. I think the cinema was called the Ritz. It was situated in the Buttermarket next to a bookshop called The Ancient House. I suppose it was a tidy walk but I do not recall it being onerous. Having crossed Stoke Bridge, we must have made out way to Silent Street, where stood the secondhand bookshop, and so on through the Eastern Counties Bus Station and along a narrow thoroughfare called Dial Lane.

I recall a badge and some form of membership and there were queues but it was all very friendly and enjoyably noisy. I have no memory of how seats were allocated, but the older girls, probably the 15 year olds, were monitors, which meant they acted as usherettes; and their task was to keep us in some kind of order. Fifteen year olds in a cinema full of excited children! But they did – more or less! There were the large photos of film stars on the walls and the cinema was actually carpeted, often in a luscious red. There was a manager who talked to us from the stage in front of a velvet curtain before the films started, and a there was a song. I can still hum the tune. The words went:

> *We are the boys and girls well known as*
> *Minors of the ABC*
> *And every Saturday we line up*

*To see the films we like
And shout aloud with glee
We love to laugh and have a singsong
Such a happy crowd are we
We're all pals together
We're minors of the ABC*

And we were a 'happy crowd' and we did 'shout aloud with glee'. I do not ever recall there being any kind of trouble. I am sure there were cartoons – *Tom and Jerry*, and *Tweety Pie* come to mind – and some old, black and white comedies – Old Mother Riley, Charlie Chaplin, Mr Pastry and Buster Keaton. There were newsreels and a feature film – Hopalong Cassidy and Roy Rogers are two I remember.

But it is the serials that stick in my mind, particularly *Flash Gordon*, *The Lone Ranger*, *Rocket Man*, *Radar Men from The Moon*, *Zorro*, and *Batman*. The serials ran for about thirteen weeks, giving us four a year. Each episode lasted no more than fifteen minutes and always ended on a cliffhanger. I remember one episode of *Flash Gordon* where he was trapped in a tank of water fighting an octopus. I barely forgave my parents if I had to miss an episode because we were going to Westerfield, and never forgave them for making me miss the final episode of *Rocket Man*.

At the end we all stood for the National Anthem. Yes, we stood quietly, no one rushed to get out before it started and we sang with it to the end. The Union Jack was fluttering, soldiers in black and red were marching and a military band was playing. Why wouldn't we? Our parents toasted the Queen's birthday and we listened to her speech on Christmas Day.

We made for the bus station after the pictures had finished because there was a fish and chip shop quite near, and it was possible to buy a pennyworth of scraps. These were the small drops of fried fat or oil that had floated to the surface during the cooking of the fish and chips, and they were delicious. We stuffed our faces with them on the way home.

One of the serials that seized our imaginations at Saturday morning pictures, 1952

The Ritz (if it was the Ritz) was one of three cinemas in Ipswich at the time; the others were the Gaumont on Major's Corner and the Odeon on Lloyd's Avenue. The Gaumont always seemed to be the posh cinema and I do not recall ever going there to see a picture. We sometimes went to the Odeon, but usually it was the Ritz, which was an ABC cinema, whatever that might mean.

Once our parents had lost any fear they might have had regarding our ventures into town, we were allowed to go to the pictures on a Saturday afternoon; but there was a huge problem.

"You can't go in the afternoon if you go in the morning," said my mother, "It isn't good for you to be in the pictures all day."

"We won't be there all day. We'll be out for lunch," I reasoned

"You'll grow up with square eyes," she replied.

"Dixie's going."

"Then Mrs Dix should know better."

It was no use arguing with my mother once her mind was made up, and the sacrifice had to be made: leave Zorro to escape from the burning hacienda without my help and go to see *Ivanhoe* with my friends who had reasonable parents.

Pictures were run continuously in the 1950s; once you were in, it was possible to sit through a film for as many times as you wished. Usually there was a B picture followed by Pathé News, which was introduced by the crowing cockerel, and then the main picture. I sat through *Ivanhoe* two-and-half times, failing to complete the third sitting because I would have been late home. Other films I remember are *The Black Shield of Falworth* (1954), *The Ten Commandments* (1956), *The Seventh Voyage of Sinbad* (1958), *Treasure Island* (1950), *Peter Pan* (1953), *Davy Crockett* (1955) and *Sleeping Beauty* (1959). These were all American-made films and all in colour. There was no doubt that the epic scale of these films was attractive and exciting. We identified with the heroes and were fascinated by the heroines – fascinated and stirred to both chivalry in their honour and desire of their femininity. I can recall my outrage at the threatened burning of Elizabeth Taylor's character, Rebecca, in *Ivanhoe* and was roused as Yul Brynner's Pharaoh proclaimed, "You will be my wife and you will bear my child" when he realised his wife-to-be loved Moses.

British films of the time included *The Dam Busters* (1954), *Carve Her Name with Pride* (1958), *The Colditz Story* (1955), *Reach for the Sky* (1956), *The Bridge over the River Kwai* (1957) and *Genevieve* (1953); only the last two were in colour. The emotions that these films stirred were admiration and patriotism. You couldn't help but believe that should you be called to fight for your country you would hold yourself as bravely and as stubbornly as these people had done.

I have researched the dates because these films span my age from six in 1950 to 15 in 1959. It seems remarkable to me, now, that I was allowed to see Treasure Island at such a tender age and it is possible that it was a repeat showing because Walt Disney films would appear every Easter. The others, however, I distinctly remember seeing when they were first shown, and with my friends because they formed the substance of many of our street and park games.

Pathé News opened up the world to us in the days before television was readily available. It was a major source of our education. The pictures were always accompanied by a rousing commentary, which seemed to be delivered each time by the same man. His voice extolled the virtues of what we were witnessing on the screen if the news was good and placed a suitable shroud over what was bad. I always felt that his opinion was the right one

Going to Saturday morning pictures also opened up the town and for me the town meant bookshops. I think that after the age of 11 my pocket money went up from sixpence a week (2.5p) to half-a-crown, which was two shillings and sixpence (12.5p). I think this because I had money in my pocket to buy books and records.

About this time, Hammer released *Dracula* (1958) which was given an X certificate as a horror film. In 1958 this meant that I would be unable to see it until I was 16 but I was fascinated. The terror of the film was heightened by an item placed in a newspaper offering a reward to anyone who would sit alone in a cinema and watch it at night. While rummaging around The Ancient House, I came across an Arrow publication of Bram Stoker's classic tale. It has one of the best covers for the story I have ever seen: the Count glares at the reader, his castle silhouetted in the background against a cloud-scudded sky, and the whole is coloured in blue tones. It was marked 'complete and unabridged' *(essential information in those days when censorship prevailed and you might end up with a book culled as considered necessary).* The cost was 2/6 – my week's pocket money! I knew my father wouldn't approve of me having the book, but it seemed to me that how I spent my pocket money was my business, and so I bought it. It was placed in the usual brown paper bag and in there I kept it, and kept it hidden to avoid the inevitable, interminable questions as to why I wanted it.

It's a little worn now but I still have the same copy, and the re-reading and re-reading of it inspired both my performance as Van Helsing in the Sewell Barn's 2010 production of a faithful play version of the story and, no doubt, my writing of The Vampire's Homecoming *(2007–09).*

I was lucky to have read the book rather than have seen the film because it is infinitely superior, although I wasn't to know this at the time. When Hammer's *The Brides of Dracula* was released in 1960, also with an X certificate, I seem to remember going to the cinema alone and without consent.

It was in The Ancient House that I also bought my first record, the MFP release of Elgar's *Enigma Variations*. Thank you m(usic)f(or)p(leasure): you made listening to music possible for those of us on 2/6 a week. Again, to avoid the incessant questions from my father as to why I wanted this record,

SATURDAY MORNING PICTURES AND GOING UP TOWN

The first book I bought for myself, 1957

I kept it hidden and played it quietly. In fact, in the beginning I didn't play it at all because I had no record player until I was sixteen or seventeen, but I enjoyed looking at the cover with its idyllic country scene. *There is always something special about the 'first of anything', and this piece of classical music is the one of the eight I would keep on my desert island.*

We wandered and idled our time to and from the pictures, up the town and around the docks. Coming home one day and stumbling across a piece of wasteland covered with brick rubble just over Stoke Bridge and up past The Bell we came across an ants nest.

"Red ants! Run! Run!" went the scream and we were off.

We hared up Bell Lane and onto Austin Street as through the Devil himself was on our heels. He might have been because red ants (whatever they might be) were the ones that bit you; red ants were the ones that could do you real harm. Laughing and screaming at the same time we imagined the terror because we needed it: it held us together in the face of danger. Our joy at this terrifying invader may have stemmed from a B movie science fiction film. I remember those but cannot, genuinely, recall their names. Only one scene comes to mind: that of a large, bulbous creature emerging from a cave. It has one extremely big eye and this looks at us with to the sound of ghostly music while waves of light shimmer around it. There are other scenes in my memory of American military personnel dashing around in jeeps, but nothing more.

'Going up town' presented its dangers: at least to our parents. The danger was not traffic, of which there was little, but Teddy Boys and Teddy Girls. They may sound cuddly through the safety of time, but in the 1950s they represented the acme of fear. There had been fights – *presumably between rival groups* – and flick knives and cut-throat razors were their reputed weapons. A primary school friend of mine, who I will call Ronnie, posed me the question: "Who would you rather be killed by – a Teddy Boy or a Teddy Girl?"

"A Teddy Girl," I said, having no real reason for the answer other than it seemed more congenial to be killed by a girl.

"You would!" he exclaimed, obviously shocked, 'I wouldn't. Teddy Girls smother you with a cushion but Teddy Boys cut your throat with a knife, and that's quicker. Being smothered to death takes a long time.'

All kinds of weapons were openly on sale in those days, and there had been fights. Teddy Boys hung around in groups and looked threatening as you passed them on a street corner, *but essentially they were fashion conscious teenagers who were unlikely to risk spoiling their expensive clothes fighting.* There was some fighting, not necessarily among the Teds but between other gangs such as the Greasers, but these were carried out with fists not knives. Using knives was considered un-English. 'Only foreigners use knives' was the accepted belief of the day.

We all carried penknives from an early age, but these were used for whittling wood and sharpening pencils. Later, when I brought up my own boys the ruling was that they passed their Cubs knife-man's badge before owning one, but that didn't apply in my childhood. I had several penknives and they were all treasured possessions, especially the one with the white, bone handle with little, embedded, silver shield.

To my shame, I once defaced a large cinema poster with a penknife. The poster was on a billboard at the bottom of Kenyon Street, near my home. I was seen by Mrs Parry, our teacher, and she hauled me over the coals about the incident in front of the class the next morning. My shame was utter and complete: I had been branded as a lout in the eyes of my peers. I felt no anger towards Mrs Parry. I needed correcting and she had made my punishment public as a warning to others on how they should behave. Sin in public; repent in public.

There was, though, little vandalism in those days. You could plan to use a public telephone knowing that the directories kept there would be intact and that the phone would be useable. There was also no graffiti: walls looked like walls and were not considered the place for filth or the province of a lout with a spray can.

Warnings from teachers about living a decent life and being wary of the company you keep were commonplace, and groups like the Teddy Boys came in for a great deal of criticism, as did the likes of Elvis Presley. Often they were grouped together for a lashing. I remember Mr Baldry being highly critical of the DA haircut.

"I saw Bailey in town on Saturday morning," he said during one assembly, "and he had this thing – this spike down the back of his hair."

The 'spike' was where the two sides of greased hair met in the semblance of a duck's arse (DA) and had been made famous by an American actor called Tony Curtis, who was the star of *The Black Shield of Falworth*. Elvis Presley had adopted this style and the older lads copied it in the days of short-back-and-sides haircuts.

Mr Baldry was genuinely concerned that adopting such a style and mixing with those who also vaunted it would lead to trouble. The boy I have called Bailey was ripe for the Teds in Mr Baldry's eyes: he attended judo classes and enjoyed fighting. He was the one who attacked the friend I went to assist; and for which action I was later caned. Bailey had twisted my arms in a judo hold while at the same time pinioning my friend to the playground.

The Elvis Presley film, Jailhouse Rock, *was released in 1957, and this, too, flagged up the warnings of a decline in moral standards.* I recall being in Mr Chittock's class at the time. One morning he was leaning back against the fireguard, the only source of heat in the room, and he proceeded to denounce the picture. Some character in the film, presumably the Presley one, had said:

"'Do unto others as you would they should do unto you – only make sure you do it first'. He is taking the words of our Lord," said Mr Chittock, "and twisting them round to give a distorted meaning."

I had not seen the film then, and haven't since, but the usual Presley film character is portrayed as a tough guy (the reason being given was that he grew up "without a Ma and Pa") but is reclaimed by the girl he loves at the end of the film. He played a similar character in Roustabout, *which I have seen.*

I don't know whether Mr Chittock had seen the film or merely read about it but in the story the Presley character is in prison for manslaughter, attacks a man while there, kisses his girl 'brutally' ("It's just the beast in me," he says), offends anyone he fails to understand, smashes his guitar and slaps his agent. It could just have been that Mr Chittock was concerned we might be impressed by such a person; in those days, our teachers had our moral welfare at heart.

We were influenced by what we saw on the big screen. I really did grow up believing that all women were like Donna Reed not just because of her performance in *It's A Wonderful Life*, which I do not remember seeing at that time, but more because of *The Donna Reed Show*. My father was against us having a television, but relented when we moved house in 1957. It was soon after, at the age of 14 or 15, I first saw this American television programme. In the show the Donna Reed character represents everything a boy moving into adolescence could dream of in a woman: she is intelligent, loving, attractive, sexy, likeable, strong, fun to be with and capable of dealing with the ups and downs of family life.

The image she portrayed was present in the other female characters we saw on the screen, on film posters in the cinemas and in film books: *King Solomon's Mines* (1950), *South Pacific* (1958), *Seven Brides for Seven Brothers* (1954) and *The King and I* (1956) portrayed an image of both femininity and masculinity that was captivating.

The girls we knew were dressed in a similar manner when we saw them at parties: puff-sleeved dresses gathered in at the waist, ribbons and bows with beautifully groomed hair styled in ringlets, held in with an Alice band. They were bright, breezy and colourful to look at and warm, funny, attractive and sassy to know.

Oh yes, we were gulled into believing what we saw on the screen, and so perhaps our schoolmasters, in their earnest concerns for our futures, had a point.

We did not, in those days, go up town to meet girls. As boys we were still emerging from childhood: we still recreated the adventures of our heroes on wasteland and street. But the girls were there: images from the screen transferred to the thoroughfares of the town.

One real excitement in town was the buses. In those days, many trolley buses still operated in Ipswich, and these had an open platform instead of a closed door. If the bus was full and people had to stand on the platform the conductor would pull the bamboo pole, used to reattach errant trolley-poles to the overhead wires, across the opening. Usually, this was not the case and, therefore, it was possible both to board and leave a trolley bus while it was in motion. This was quite a skill because it relied on your judgement of the speed of the bus. I have never been particularly athletic but I did master this art. We would go to the platform before the bus reached its stop and at the right moment swing out easily onto the street. Often, we would wait for a bus to leave the stop before boarding, and then run after it, catching the support at the right moment and leaping on.

People queued in a very orderly manner, and a man would always step back to allow a lady who happened to be behind him to get on first. There was no danger of finding a dirty seat because people simply did not put their feet on the seats: had they done so the conductor would soon have had a word with them

The conductor kept order on the bus and collected the fares. He was also in control of stopping and starting the bus. When everyone was seated he would call out:

"Hold tight, please."

He would then ring the bell and walk along the bus collecting the fares. Most had a machine that held tickets of different values marked by a different colour. Once you had told him where you wanted to go, the conductor would press down a small lever that released the correct ticket. Having taken your money, he dropped it into a large leather bag that hung from a strap round his shoulders.

My Uncle Ken worked on the buses, and boarding his bus ensured maximum embarrassment because he would let you travel without paying. He seemed to know that this was humiliating because he would look you directly in the eyes, pretend to release a ticket and hand it to you without taking the money that was clutched in your sweaty hand. He would then engage you in a conversation concerning family matters.

"How's your mum? Is your dad all right? Florrie's got a bit of a cold, and so she's not too happy at the moment ..."

With everyone listening, this kind of talk ensured you left the bus blushing furiously.

I remember arriving back home on one occasion to be told by my mother that a Mrs Bird, who lived nearly opposite us on Turin Street had called me "a little snob" because I hadn't spoken to her when travelling on the same bus. I hadn't seen her as it happened, and it occurred to me that since she had seen and ignored me she was the snob, if the term applied at all. I almost pointed this out to my mother but refrained from doing so, knowing that it would be seen as disrespectful.

Was this an early lesson in taking no notice of what people think of you or say about you? Yes, it was and I realised that at the time. It took many more years, however, before I understood that people who speak about others in that way are actually talking about themselves.

Name calling among us children was quite common, and it was not always as spiteful as it may appear. 'Tubby', as I explained in relation to my Uncle Eric, was not intended as an offensive term for fat people because it was not thought shameful to be fat. Likewise, 'Shorty' or 'Tich' were more or less terms of endearment for small people and 'Lanky' or 'Slim' a compliment to someone tall. 'Ginger' described a red haired person and 'Specs' someone who wore glasses. If offence was intended then the terminology and tone made it clear: hence, 'fatso', 'four-eyes' and 'snotty' were used against an enemy but never a friend.

Nicknames have always been common in Suffolk, and I was always 'Canty'. Sometimes a nickname would refer to a physical attribute such as hair: so blonde hair generated 'Blondie' and curly hair 'Curly'. Someone who missed nothing was often called 'Hawkeye', anyone with the name Brown was 'Brownie', a Clarke or a Norman was always 'Nobby' ... and so on.

It was quite rare that we went up town with our parents. If we did, it was usually to buy new clothes for school. Shoes were always an exciting purchase. My mother would only 'fit us out with the best' and so we went to the Clarke's shop in the Buttermarket. Here, they had an X-ray machine, and so you could see how much 'growing room' there was in the pair you had bought. The machine was a large one and it was necessary to stand with your feet in the gap and look down through the top; bones and all were clearly visible, and so you left with a pair that was too big at first but which 'you would grow into' and be made comfortable in the meantime by an insole. My father was forever harping on about 'brogues', which were a type of leather shoe with patterns on the top and a bar dividing the main upper from the toecap. These shoes 'lasted forever', which was rather pointless for a growing child. Most shoes had to be 'worn in', which meant months of agonising discomfort until wearing them had softened the leather. Shoes were cleaned and polished everyday 'to preserve the leather'. My mother did this at night until I was old enough to spread Cherry Blossom shoe polish over the kitchen floor for myself.

Likewise, school clothes, which ended up as play clothes, were always bought to 'allow room to grow into', and so there was only ever a brief moment of time when they actually fitted: for the first term they were too big and by the summer had become excruciatingly tight, but not too tight to end up as play clothes the following autumn.

One huge delight of going up town with Mum, however, was dropping off at the Lyon's Tea Shop or at Footman's for afternoon tea. Footman's was a department store with old-fashioned lifts: the type with the internal cage door as well as the outer main door. There was also a lift attendant who would call out the floor number as you arrived. On the top floor was a very posh teashop, where waitresses attended your table in black dresses and a natty white apron, frilled and tied neatly with a bow at the back. Mum would order: "Tea for two, please."

This would come with a selection of cakes on one of those triple-layered cake stands, bread and butter, sometimes scones with jam and cream, together with tea in a teapot, matching china cups and a jug of hot water to top up the teapot. This was a real treat in a decade of shortages and rationing.

Chapter 10
Festivities and Holidays

Christmas was quieter then than it is now, but just as special. We did not expect expensive gifts, and we were not disappointed; moderation was the order of the day, and I think it was in line with the real meaning of Christmas.

My mother did not decorate until Christmas Eve, and so it was a wonder and a surprise when we came down on Christmas morning. The little tree always stood in the corner where my Triang desk usually held sway, and it was always decorated in precisely the same manner. *There was nothing boring in this exactitude; it was the continuation of a tradition that stemmed back to when my mother was a young wife.* The tree sported real candles and these were always lit when we came for our presents. Taffeta hung from the branches, pine cones were sited in their customary places, snow bedecked the green of the pine and the fairy ruled the topmost bough. In later years, Mum must have bought, at considerable expense, a set of lights whose shades were illustrated with characters from nursery rhymes – I still have them, and illuminate them at some risk each Christmas – and these, replacing the candles, were the central focus of the tree.

I remember Mum watching as we emerged from the doorway of the stairs that led down from the bedrooms; she was eager that we should be enchanted, and we were. Our stockings hung from the fireplace where Father Christmas had filled them, and those presents too large for the stockings were placed in the hearth. He must have enjoyed the glass of sherry and the mince pie we left for him because the glass was empty and only crumbs remained on the plate. The 'stockings' were, in fact, pillow cases, and they did hold a considerable number of gifts: the *Rupert* annual, the clockwork train set, the jigsaw puzzle, the board game, the metal or plastic puzzle and, at the very bottom, the bar of chocolate, the nuts and the oranges; always the nuts and the oranges to remind us how lucky we were to live where we did.

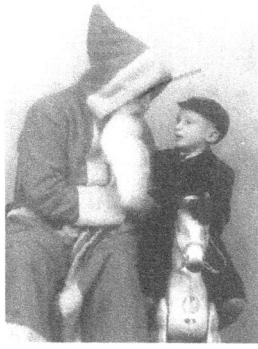

With Father Christmas, probably in Footman's Department Store, c 1949

Mum had already lit the fire and so we unwrapped our presents in comfort. I cannot remember whether it was before or after breakfast, but Dad would have wanted his traditional fried meal come what may. Later, I can remember the 'stocking' being placed at the foot of my bed, but the upstairs rooms were cold and we must have carried our presents down to be opened. We would have had to wait for Mum and Dad to wake up if our excitement roused us early, and I can recall finding a plastic trumpet one year and giving it a blast at the top of the stairs, calling out: "And here, everybody, is Eddie Calvert!"

Dad was not overly impressed and bundled me back to bed.

We were always dressed in our Sunday best on Christmas Day, and were never allowed outside to play, even if the present was a scooter, which I had one year. It was considered bad form to be on the street on Christmas Day in much the same way as it was considered common to play out on Sunday. Apart from visits to our grandparents, the only outside attraction was likely to be Billy Smart's or Bertram Mill's Circus on Christchurch Park and this was a momentous night out, usually on one of the days following Christmas.

Christmas dinner was very like our traditional Sunday roast, but with the extra balls of stuffing, and with a cracker lined up against the cutlery. We always had chicken on Christmas Day. It was a special treat because chicken was an expensive meat. This would have been a farm-reared bird: strong, tangy meat and sinewy legs but cooked to a turn. Dessert, or afters as we called it, was a Christmas pudding, which I loved, and so Mum kept one aside as a treat for my birthday. Always in the pudding was an old, silver three-penny bit, and always it was us children who found it.

The dinner was finished by three o'clock when we sat round the radio and listened to the Queen's Speech. When the National Anthem played, we all stood, and my dad stood very much to attention.

The afternoon was spent playing one of the board games we had received as a present. Full of food, the grown-ups sometimes dozed by the fire but would come around to a game eventually.

Christmas tea was often a get together with Nana and Grandad Bathstreet, and then the cake was cut. The knife slid through the royal icing, carefully avoiding the Christmas tree, the boy on the sledge and the robin – decorations that appeared year after year.

Christmas had, in fact, begun a few weeks earlier when the man himself arrived in the local department store. His grotto was, quite literally, an ice cave. I recall making my way, alone because Mum could only go so far, along a winding corridor of silver, glistening ice; and there he was, waiting on his throne-like chair for me to tell him what I wanted for Christmas. One year, when Dad was away at sea, we sent him a photograph of me with Father Christmas. How that came to be taken I have no idea, but it is now in the family album.

The shop windows, especially those in the town centre, were always decorated especially for Christmas. The Salvation Army band would dominate the main street with its brass music; I remember hearing it from the Cornhill to the White Horse Hotel. Festive lights were strung everywhere. I can remember Mum going from shop to shop after the different items she would require for the big day and there abided with us an almost siege mentality. Everything had to be bought before the day itself but as late as possible so that it 'wouldn't go off'. Queues were a part of this frenzied shopping, not so much in the town stores but certainly in the local ones: queues for the butchers, the grocers, the greengrocers and the bakers. Buy too early and the food would perish, and there was no chance to buy too late because the shops would be closed for the Christmas season.

Mum produced a lot of her own foodstuffs. Prior to the day, over the months of autumn, there had been much bottling and pickling and preserving: vegetables and fruits, chutneys and relishes, jams and marmalades. It was a time when Kilner jars came into their own. She also made the cake, the puddings, the mince pies and the sausage rolls.

Drink would have been Dad's responsibility, but I remember very little of it being in the house: perhaps a bottle of port and one of sherry, but that would be all and may well have been kept in the sideboard since the previous year.

All this happened as if by magic rather than hard work. We were only aware of the bustle in passing, just as we were only aware of Christmas a short time before. The decorations on Christmas morning were only one surprise; another would be the sudden sound of carol singers on Turin Street. We would pass through the front room and listen before opening the door and dropping a few coppers in their collection box.

Christmas Day was parsimonious because times were hard and people were finding it difficult to make ends meet and not because of any religious objection to materialism. Apart from its presence on Christmas cards and decorations, the spiritual side of the day figured very little in our celebrations at home. Schools provided this element through stories, nativity plays, books and pictures. Schools also gave us a chance to tap into our creative side in making decorations, cards and calendars. Excitement was intense as we were given strips of gummed paper, which we moistened, folded into a circle and linked with others to make a paper chain. Each child's chain was joined to the others, and so a ten link chain soon became four hundred, and was enough to string across and round the classroom. We made a calendar for Mum and a card for both Mum and Dad.

Music played its part in our Christmas celebrations, even if it was limited to a tap on a triangle but it was always the singing that caught my imagination both at primary and secondary school. I found no difficulty with the archaic words of traditional hymns. Phrases like 'risen with healing in his wings', 'mild he lays his glory by', 'all meanly wrapped in swaddling bands', brighter visions beam afar', 'where meek souls will receive him still' and 'still through the cloven skies they come' carry sufficient meaning in their poetry to overcome the need to make immediate sense of them. At primary school we sang to a piano; at secondary school to the organ in St Margaret's Church, having rehearsed with Mr Baldry on both piano and harmonium. Mrs Parry told me at primary school that I had no singing voice, but there is a world of difference between singing solo and singing in a group; and everyone can sing carols.

Each class had its own party: jelly, fairy cakes, popular songs like *Rudolf the Red-nosed Reindeer*, pass the parcel and musical chairs. Christmas celebrations brought us together in a shared enjoyment of the season. Whether it was the stories or the music or the craftwork or the drama, it gave us a time in the year to which we could look forward and a time when we could all contribute.

In 1953, Queen Elizabeth the Second was crowned in Westminster Abbey, and we all enjoyed a street party. Territorial

FESTIVITIES AND HOLIDAYS

rights were set aside for the big occasion and long tables were set out in Pauline Street. I must have known what the party was in aid of but even if I hadn't the atmosphere was, as they say, electric. Sweets had come off the ration in time for the Coronation (although they went back on afterwards) and we all stuffed ourselves silly. There were no paper plates in those days, thank God, and so we all enjoyed eating from the real McCoy: food on plates, squash in glasses. Where they came from I have no idea, as I have no idea who did the washing up.

Paper plates, anyway, would have been out of place on the pristine white linen tablecloths, under street lamp-posts decorated in red, white and blue and watched over by Union Jacks hung from windows along the street.

A few people had bought their first television for the occasion, but only a few, and so people crammed into, perhaps, one or two houses of their neighbours to watch the Queen process to the Abbey on the tiny black and white screens. There was no envy then, despite the general hardship. People looked on it as a day of celebration for all, rich or poor.

School photograph, Coronation Year, 1953

We boys had our hair cut for the occasion – short back and sides – and were dressed in our Sunday best – in my case, a child's version of a grownups suit but with short trousers – and the girls had on a best dress, probably homemade, and ribbons in their hair. The mothers had taken the trouble to place flowers in vases along the centre of the table, and we were all given a Coronation mug to take home.

Bonfire Night was always special. Dad was highly organised and had a fixture for every firework: buckets of sand for the Roman candles, a length of pipe attached to a sturdy baseboard at an angle of 60 degrees for the rockets, a four by four garden post sharpened at one end and hammered into the ground for the Catherine wheels. He always set the fireworks off in our back garden both at Turin Street and Gleneagles Drive. Everyone let off their own fireworks and so the back passageway was a plethora of festive lights. There was no problem buying the fireworks: us children simply took the money to Mr and Mrs Whales at the corner shop and paid over the counter. Choosing them was always exciting because the money was limited and selecting the most illustrious ones was essential. Once we were living at Gleneagles Drive we also had a bonfire, although Turin Street had been too small for one.

The bonfire for Turin Street was a neighbourhood event, long before such things became popular for safety reasons, and there was nothing particularly safe about the bonfire in Austin Street. It must have stood anything up to thirty feet high, and was built in the centre of a large stretch of wasteland covered with the rubble of derelict houses. The local youths had collected every item they could find that would burn from early in the autumn. One lanky youth seemed to be the self-appointed protector of the bonfire, and he would chase off anyone who got too near; if he caught you, it was a thick ear for your impertinence in approaching the near-sacred object. Your only chance of getting close was by bringing something to burn. One year I saw a pram on top of the heap and in the pram sat a Guy. I could never work out how it got there! Once it was lit, the stack went up like a torch and could not have failed to scorch the windows and doors of neighbouring houses. Sparks and debris flew everywhere, up and over rooftops and away into the night.

We made our own Guys, and Mum was very good in providing old clothes and helping us stitch them together. Once made, they would be placed in an old pram or pushchair or carried around the neighbourhood.

"Penny for the Guy, mister?" we begged.

Some people tossed a copper into our hat; others said: "Buzz off!"

It was all good fun, although Mum did not like us begging. Some kids did not make a Guy, but dirtied their faces and flopped out on the pavements while their friends did the begging. I thought this was cheating at the time because they had made no effort in return for the money begged; *but I have changed my mind with age, seeing that they were acting for a living.*

When Dad was stationed at HMS *Ganges,* Shotley, the navy put on a firework display and bonfire of their own. We would go down on the bus to watch and the pyrotechnics were always dazzling and impressive; but we watched from afar and sometimes from an upstairs window of the base to get a good view and it lacked the immediacy of our own back garden display.

I always enjoyed bonfire night, and this enjoyment carried on through the years in which I raised my own family and we had our display and large bonfire in our back garden, attended by many friends. The snapping and crackling of the fire, the various exploding lights of the fireworks, the smell of sulphur in the air, the thick plumes of smoke rising into the night sky and the taste of a jacket potato were all part of the magic and an essential part of the evening.

Holidays were centred in or around the home and days out to the seaside; if we went further afield it was to a relative or a friend. One such day was to visit two of my mother's maiden aunts at Clopton; they were the sisters of her mother, Anna-Maria, and their names were May and Nell. The term

'English country' was coined to describe their garden: stretching from the rickety gate to the front door of their adjoining thatched cottages were purple-leaved violas, double daisies, aquilegia, peonies, sage, meadow rue, campanula, gypsophila and many other plants whose names I have long forgotten. Aunt May's door opened onto a front parlour with its beamed ceiling and its petite settee with floral covers. A small table, served by two wooden chairs, stood under the lattice window, whose sill contained potted plants. In one corner of the fireplace with its black wrought-iron dog crate stood a grandfather clock and in the other was the door leading upstairs. Another door opened onto the tiny kitchen, and through the window of this the back garden could be glimpsed. A kettle hissed on the hob by the fire.

Aunt May served tea precisely at four o'clock and it was her custom to knock on the wall between her parlour and Nell's at this hour.

"I'm having my tea now, Nell," she would say, and back came an answering tap.

"I'm having my tea, too, May."

They would then both sit in their own front parlour enjoying their tea, together but apart.

When we visited, it was always to Aunt May's cottage that we went, and we shared her tea: a few rounds of bread and butter with jam she had made from fruit of the previous year, perhaps a slice of fruit cake with tea for Mum and lemonade for us children. We only saw Nell as we left to catch the bus, when she would appear from her own front door and wave us goodbye. We usually departed with an armful of rhubarb or some summer fruits. We were given a share of whatever was in season: raspberries, gooseberries, apples or pears.

A trip to the seaside – usually Felixstowe – demanded a degree of organisation worthy of a safari tour operator. Everything needed had to be carried, and I have described the effort involved in chapter 4. Felixstowe was accessible by bus or by train and I think we usually went by bus.

Lorna, Edna, and Fred's families with Nana and Grandad Bathstreet on Felixstowe beach

Wearing one's ordinary clothes on the beach was not a matter of choice, since there was no choice: they were the only clothes we possessed. They would have been the smart ones – our Sunday best – and we had to look our best. A jacket might be removed if it was hot but rarely the tie, and a short-sleeved pullover was mandatory. We took off our summer sandals to paddle, and the grownups either held tight to their dresses or rolled up their trouser legs. I never saw my parents in a swimming costume but we children did have one: the woollen trunks I have already described in the case of us boys. Some of my aunts must, as the 50s wore on, have changed their habits because I can remember those rubber bathing caps, often decorated with flower and shell shapes, but I cannot picture my mother in the water.

We enjoyed ourselves making sandcastles (at which my dad was a dab hand), digging deep holes and burying ourselves up to our necks, and enjoying the real treat of an ice cream or lollypop. I think we children entertained ourselves a great deal on the beach, and that the grownups (who had made the huge effort to get us there) saw it as a chance to have a rest. They looked for a place by the sea wall or a breakwater so they could rest their backs. I think I only once saw my father with a knotted handkerchief on his head, but this was a common enough sight; the idea that someone might buy a sunhat was frowned upon as a waste of money. After all, how many times were you going to use it?

Deckchairs could be hired from an attendant who kept a pile by his hut on the promenade. He always wore a peaked cap with a white cover and carried a large leather bag like those used by bus conductors. A large family party would hire only a few deckchairs and these would be for the grandparents; people of my parents' age would sit on the beach, legs outstretched.

I remember a pier, but I cannot say whether or not this was at Felixstowe. It was equipped with slot machines and telescopes through which you could look out to sea. The slot machines contained challenges. If you were lucky, you might manoeuvre a stack of coins so that one fell into a trough where you could collect it, or you might wield the shovel at the end of a toy crane and pick up a bar of chocolate or a small cuddly toy. On the beach there were donkey rides and the Punch and Judy show, and Mum would always buy a picture postcard from one of the stalls on the promenade to send to her mother or to an aunt. Alongside these postcards of the place were those with cartoon drawings of little husbands being bawled at by big wives or women with sumptuous breasts wondering why the bloke with them was dazed. It was adult humour and held little interest for us children.

My mum and my aunts always looked attractive in their flowered summer dresses, whether sitting on the beach, looking for postcards or going to buy the ice-creams. One of us children always went with them because the ice cream was likely to be running down the side of the cornet if it wasn't

FESTIVITIES AND HOLIDAYS

hurried back to the crowd on the beach. I can recall nipping sharply back to the family group, three cornets in each hand, frantically licking round each one to stop the ice cream dripping over my hands.

On the beach at
Dovercourt, 1949

With Linda on a visit to our
godparents in Westcliffe

Sometimes we travelled further afield but only to relatives. My godparents, Aunty Molly and Uncle Ernie, lived at Westcliffe-on-Sea and we did spend time with them and with my Uncle Albert and his wife who lived at Dovercourt.

My godparents were the ones who introduced me to at least two of the classics: *David Copperfield* and *Kidnapped*. When I went to my bedroom, the top sheet and blanket were turned back and a copy of the book lay on the pillow. Even on holiday, I must have read a great deal. We were left to our own devices and without friends from home or television; books were an ideal answer to what would otherwise have been hours of boredom. I can honestly say that I have never been bored: the imaginary worlds created by writers in their stories have always been home to me.

Travelling to such places as these involved journeying by train – steam trains with their smuts and dirty carriages. Railway stations, themselves, were cold, unwelcoming places with the perpetual presence of smoke, steam and the smell of oil; there was always a draught somewhere on a railway station whether you were standing on the platform or bundled into the waiting room.

I didn't actually mind the carriages despite the grubby seats because there was a fascination in the sash windows that could be raised and lowered using a leather strap, there was the emergency chain – IN CASES OF EMERGENCY PULL DOWN THE CHAIN – and there was the corridor, which meant that you could walk the length of the train pretending you were going to the toilet. There was something very exciting about keeping one's balance in the corridor of a moving train.

I was always puzzled by the lack of second-class carriages. There was a first class for the posh people and a third class for the rest of us, but why wasn't there a second class for the doctors, the bank clerks, the teachers, the nurses and the people who worked in the Town Hall? In those days, you could buy a platform ticket to see people off on their train. During those days in the summer when I was trainspotting we would buy such a ticket and watch trains go by on the station platform; it was never a great interest of mine but David Garnham, my Aunt Betty's eldest son, once persuaded me to go to Manningtree station and we enjoyed ourselves.

We did go away for a whole week once to Kessingland, which is about forty miles north of Ipswich, where we stayed in a caravan. We must have travelled by train to Lowestoft and then caught the local bus because Dad had no car at that time. Caravan sites were quite popular because they offered a relatively cheap holiday, but for us it was a disaster. To begin with we did not get the caravan Dad had requested, and much time was spent justifying his decision to accept one that Mum and he obviously considered inferior. At the age I was that summer, which must have been fifteen, I was old enough to appreciate the tensions that can exist between a husband and wife over such matters. I can remember wondering why they didn't just accept the situation or decide to go home. Neither of them was happy with their decision and their disgruntlement rubbed off onto Linda and me.

Our caravan holiday at Kessingland, circa 1958

I could tell that Mum and Dad were aware of this because he kept trying to bring us in on the conversations, but I wasn't having any of it. I had already learned that to get involved in such conflicts was disastrous: somewhere along the line, blame would be apportioned and it wasn't going to fall on me. I just kept wishing that we could get out of the caravan and on to the beach. Looking back, I do not think that Mum was keen on such a holiday: she liked to have her house around her, and making do in a caravan was not her cup of tea.

Eventually, we did get out and enjoyed a week rambling along the dunes to the inland lakes, and following the clifftop to Covehithe. I had my first dog, Kim, who was a Cairn terrier, with me and he had the time of his life chasing the rabbits into their warrens. He splashed in the sea, chased sticks and balls and explored Kessingland's many beaches: the dunes, the sands, the pebbles.

Funnily enough, the place where I ended the decade was the place where, eventually, my own sons spent their childhood, and they must have enjoyed it. One said that his childhood may have been a rose garden; another wrote and thanked his mother and me for his childhood, saying 'thanks for my childhood: it couldn't have been better'; and my youngest wrote that 'it was nice to be part of a family that enjoyed being together'. Perhaps, after all, I had learned something on that caravan holiday because my son's mother and I never aired our differences in front of them and at their expense when they were children.

Kessingland was as far as we went unless we stayed with relatives. Most of the long, glorious, summer holiday – a time treasured so much by families because it gives them time to be together – was spent in much the same way as our weekends and evenings: on the streets, in the neighbourhood, exploring the area.

We had good weather (wasn't every day sunny?) and long days stretching into the light evenings. Days out to the parks or along the Strand were more leisurely. Local fairs visited sometimes and we would be given extra money to spend that day. One summer, go-karting was the craze and Dixie's dad made him one, which he shared. We even dared to make our way onto Littles Crescent to give us that extra speed to fly down Vaughan Street, past Pauline Street and Turin Street, to swerve to a halt as we came to Wherstead Road where the bus might pass.

Dads were at work, of course, but our Mums were always around to tend cut knees and bloody noses, and provide us with breakfast, dinner and tea. They would always emerge from their front doors to call us in, although we somehow knew the time instinctively.

At quiet moments we might sit on the pavements playing five stones or take cover in Dixie's dad's workshop to plan what our gang might do next. Crazes for collecting gathered momentum and cigarette cards and bubble gum cards would be swapped and stuck into their respective albums. If our pocket money had been spent, we would scour the dumps for metal and take it to the scrap yard.

In the 1950s we were left very much to our own devices. We were used to amusing ourselves and always found something to do.

Chapter 11
Moving Out

In the garden of our new bungalow at Gleneagles Drive, 1958

In 1957 an event occurred that was to mark and change my life: my parents moved house. The friends of my childhood who would have become the friends of my adolescence were lost to me forever. I had school friends, of course, but since St Margaret's had no designated catchment area they were scattered across the town. *There is much to be said for a child attending their catchment area school; in that way they remain close to their neighbourhood friends.* I found myself on a new housing development where I knew no one, and I became a loner. Living over Stoke, I returned to my natural friends each night; living on the edge of Rushmere Heath, I returned to no one of my own age.

It was soon after this move that my parents bought me my bicycle and my dog: the first gave me a degree of freedom to move about more easily than using public transport would have done and the second gave me instant companionship.

We wandered the heath together as far as it ranged, which in those days must have extended almost as far as Bell Lane. Here, we entered an area of woodland, dominated by the beautiful silver birch, which bordered on the entrance to the sanatorium, where, previously, children suffering from tuberculosis had been quarantined. Acres of land were ours: bracken, streams and wild birds. I learned a great deal from Kim. I learned that dogs have a natural loyalty to their companion and do not need to be trained. They will come where they are loved. On one occasion, my father took him for a walk and Kim refused to come when called. My father stormed off the heath – chin up, chest out, shoulders back in true naval fashion – and informed me that my dog had not been trained properly. I went after him, dropped to my knees and he ran to me without a murmur.

"You had to get down on your knees to get him back," said my father.

He was missing the point. The dog was frightened of his authoritarian manner, but would come to one he loved and trusted. *Dropping down on your knees isn't a sign of submission, but of being at one with those over whom you have a charge; it is the sign of the leader. My father could not know that but I did; I knew it then as I know it now.*

But Kim, wonderful though he was and grateful as I am for all I learned from being with him, was not a human companion, and of those I was bereft.

True, I cycled out to meet my school friends at the weekends and during the summer evenings but when I walked to our new gate at night I was alone in the world.

The outside world was opened in 1957, quite unexpectedly, when my father, protesting loudly that "it would kill the art of conversation", allowed us to have a television set. (Another seven years were to pass before he considered a telephone to be necessary.) I remember vividly the day it was installed. The retailer, Matthews of Foxhall Road, sent his technician to set it up. My father was insistent that we should not have an aerial on the roof "because they blight the neighbourhood and make it ugly", and so the technician had to assemble the huge H-shaped contraption in the loft. This resulted in a picture that was more several shades of grey than black and white, but it was an improvement on nothing. My mother, sister and I, together with my father, sat glued to the 12 inch screen waiting for something to appear as the technician nipped up and down the loft ladder adjusting the aerial, wiggled and juggled the knobs of the television and moved the box back and forth, left and right, until a picture did appear.

I think my sister and I benefitted most from this modern innovation into our home. On a Sunday afternoon, in particular, while my father tapped on the lounge window telling us there were stones to be picked off the garden, we enjoyed a host of old films. I think I watched *Mr Blandings Builds His Dream House* (1948) with Cary Grant and Myrna Loy at least three times. It must have been here, also, that we first saw the gangster movies featuring stars like James Cagney, Edward G Robinson and George Raft. The box in the corner also gave us a chance to see those British films that we had missed at the cinema: films like *The Man in the White Suit* (1951), *The Card* (1952) and *The Pickwick Papers* (1952). I can also remember a great number of Fred Astaire and Ginger Rogers' films and biopics about people like Cole Porter.

There were other joys in the series that came regularly to our little screen. There were the drama series: *The Buccaneers* (1956) about a band of pirates led by Dan Tempest; *Dixon of Dock Green* (1956) about old-style policing; *Emergency Ward 10* (1957) a light drama about life in a hospital; *Ivanhoe* (1958) that starred Roger Moore; *The Adventures of Robin*

Hood (1955) stealing, light-heartedly, from the rich to give to the poor.

There were the comedy series: *The Army Game* (1957) a comedy about National Service; *The Arthur Haynes Show* (1956) that boasted some surreal sketches, unusual at the time; *Hancock's Half Hour* (1956) that featured the comedian, Tony Hancock, along with a team of regulars.

The entertainment shows: *The Black and White Minstrel Show* (1958) that introduced Dixieland songs; *Juke Box Jury* (1959) that introduced pop music judged by a panel; *Sunday Night at the London Palladium* (1955) a must-see show that held us glued to the set each week; *Six-Five Special* (1957) that gave us rock 'n' roll and jazz; *This is Your Life* (1955) that featured highlights of the lives of well-known people.

The children's programmes: *Blue Peter* (1958) that was intended for young children but held us all; *Captain Pugwash* (1957) a cartoon adventure that often rounded off children's viewing for the evening.

The American innovations: *77 Sunset Strip* (1958) about a team of private investigators; *Perry Mason* (1957) an American lawyer/detective drama; *The Phil Silvers Show* (1957) that featured the American comedian as wise-cracking sergeant, Bilko, on an American forces base; *Wagon Train* (1958) made its way across our screens and the deserts of America in hour-long episodes.

Watching television did much more than entertain: it opened up further worlds and led us back into the classics of literature. The BBC adaptations of Charles Dickens's stories, which were often broadcast close to teatime on a Sunday, introduced me to his writings. These were serial adaptations that kept you glued to the screen for months at a time.

But the world of television is an unreal world; it is a world that lacks human contact, and – as I have said – I was without friends of my own age. If you cannot turn out, you turn in and I turned to books.

As a child, with my mother, I had listened to the radio and to 'Carleton Hobbs as Sherlock Holmes and Norman Shelley as Dr

Watson'. Now, I turned to the stories themselves. The first book I bought – with its striking red, yellow and brown illustration on the cover of Holmes standing under a gaslight – was *The Adventures of Sherlock Holmes*, and I devoured every story.

Years later, when I tried to interest my sons in the Holmes stories all I received was a look of scorn that I could ever have believed them to be mysteries and ever admired Holmes's cleverness; but my sons were more intelligent and more knowledgeable than I was at their age and, perhaps, their reaction should have been expected.

TEACH YOURSELF

SELF-DEFENCE

By

ERIC DOMINY
(Black Belt Holder and British International)

Illustrated by

PETER JOHNSON

THE ENGLISH UNIVERSITIES PRESS LTD
102, NEWGATE STREET,
LONDON, E.C.1.

Inspired by the Sherlock Holmes stories,
I bought this book in 1957

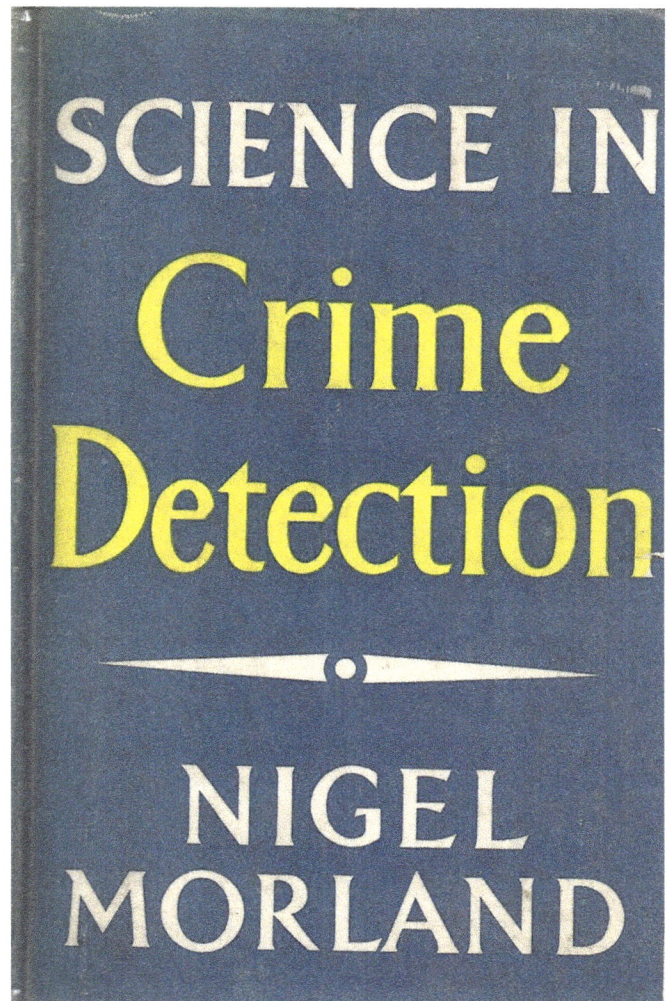

Inspired by the Sherlock Holmes stories,
I bought this book in 1958

To me, they opened up another world: the world of the gifted amateur and the world of forensic science. I read every book on which I could lay hands: Nigel Morland's *Science in Crime Detection* was one, and I dreamed of being a scientist, while knowing that the dream was fruitless. The 11+ exam had placed me beyond science; there was no chance that I could catch up on my studies – even had I known where to study – in order to gain the necessary grades at 'O' level to be accepted on an 'A' level course. Anyway, what were 'O' levels or 'A' levels? At 13 I had heard of neither.

Apart from leading me into forensic science, the Sherlock Holmes' stories also opened up Conan Doyle's other works and interests. I read the Professor Challenger stories, particularly *The Lost World, The Poison Belt* and *The Land of Mist*. The first of these awakened an interest in dinosaurs, evolution and, eventually, the work of Charles Darwin; the second led me into science fiction: Verne, Wells, Wyndham and other 50s' SF writers; the third into the paranormal and psychical research: spiritualism telepathy, clairvoyance, mediumship, psychokinesis, apparitions, hauntings and out-of-body experiences. After Holmes' fight with Moriarty at the Reichenbach Falls, I studied self-defence through a book in the Teach Yourself series by Eric Dominy. Conan Doyle himself, through his interests in the George Edalji and Oscar Slater cases, persuaded me to research famous trials. But these interests were without order or a basic, fundamental knowledge of the subjects and sciences on which a thorough understanding might rest.

I was adrift in a world of intellect and knowledge without a guide and without a compass. My secondary school teachers, who I have mentioned in chapter 6, were an inspiration but charting a purposeful course in a muddled educational world was impossible. Fortunately, two years, later, at the age of 15, I was washed ashore at the Ipswich Civic College and there – late in the day but very welcome – I found some of the help I needed: Oswald Job (History), Dickie Worsnop (again) (Mathematics), Mr Youngs (General Science), Martin Lewis (Geography), Diane Grace (English), Tom Parry (English), Bill Boaden (Geography) and Noel Boaden (Geography) were some of the great lecturers who refitted my ship and helped it steer a course to a more fulfilling destination. They gave me my 'O' and 'A' levels and soaked up some of the angst I felt;

for their knowledge, expertise, experience and patience I am eternally grateful. I was then and I am now.

On a field study trip from the Ipswich Civic College 1962

It was socially where I was most isolated, and this is probably one of the reasons why I have never had any real feeling for pop music, then or now. *I think you can always judge how important a song was to you at the time by whether or not you remember the words a few years later.* Casting my mind back to the 50s, I remember most of Lonnie Donegan's songs, especially *Rock Island Line* (1954), *John Henry* (1955), *Stewball* (1956), *Cumberland Gap* (1957), *Puttin' on the Style* (1957), *Great Grand Coulee Dam* (1958) and *Kevin Barry* (1959); Cliff Richard's *Travellin' Light* (1959) was a firm favourite, along with Chris Barber's *Petite Fleur* (1959), Tommy Steele's *Singing the Blues* (1956), Tony Bennett's *Stranger in Paradise* (1955), the Everly Brothers' *All I Have To Do Is Dream* (1958), Buddy Holly's *I Guess It Doesn't Matter Anymore* (1959) and Jerry Lee Lewis's *Great Balls of Fire* (1957); but I remember little of anything else of the here-and-now chart topping music.

It wasn't until I went to teacher training college in 1963 that the great blues, jazz, rock 'n' roll and country singers came my way, along with Bob Dylan and Paul Simon; and by then my adolescence had come and gone.

This lack of interest in popular music both fed and was a product of my social isolation. I took no interest in teenage (*a new word in the 50s*) fashion, never used trendy words like 'cool', 'cat' or 'square', never gathered with my friends in coffee bars (Ipswich had a famous one called The Gondoliers in Upper Orwell Street), never hung around a juke-box, was never tempted to smoke as a mark of rebellion, never went to local football matches.

There was an innocence about me as the 50s came to a close: an innocence I was to carry like a weight on my shoulders for several years.

                              Ipswich, Suffolk   1944 – 1959
                              Loddon, Norfolk   2015

www.ingramcontent.com/pod-product-compliance
Lightning Source LLC
Chambersburg PA
CBHW040315170426
43196CB00020B/2925